Unveiled

Autobiography of an
Awakened One

Dawn James

ublish and Promote

Unveiled

Autobiography of an
Awakened One

ISBN 978-1-9995564-7-1 Paperback
ISBN 978-1-9995564-8-8 ePUB
ISBN 978-1-9995564-9-5 Audiobook

Edited by Christine Bode
Design and layout by Perseus Design
Cover design by David Moratto

Publish and Promote
DawnJames.ca
PublishandPromote.ca

Note to the reader: The events in this book are based on my memory from my perspective. Certain names have been changed to protect the identity of those mentioned. The information is provided for educational purposes only. In the event you use any of the information in this book for yourself, which is your constitutional right, the author and publisher assume no responsibility for your actions.

Printed and bound in Canada.

Other Books and Audiobooks
by Dawn James

Raise Your Vibration, Transform Your Life (English, Spanish)
https://www.amazon.com/Dawn-James/e/B003BAIT7W

How to Raise the Vibration Around You
https://www.amazon.com/Dawn-James/e/B003BAIT7W

Raise the Vibration Between Us
(English, Spanish, French, Hindi)
https://www.amazon.com/Dawn-James/e/B003BAIT7W

Raise the Vibration Between Us (audiobook)
https://dawnjames.ca/raise-the-vibration-between-us-audio/

Why Are We Here (audiobook)
https://dawnjames.ca/why-are-we-here/

Dedication

This book is dedicated to my parents, whose divine connection gave me life. They were my first spiritual teachers in their unique way, and I am grateful they taught me how to be resilient and to navigate the twists, turns, and bumps in the road of my two lives.

Contents

Foreword

by Michael Moon, Astrologer

I have always loved autobiographies. I love deep diving into another life and another perspective on life. Usually, we are drawn to famous personalities and what makes them tick but what about the average person walking the path next to you? When we look deeply, we see that all lives encounter lessons and are filled with drama and beauty. I have known Dawn for many years as a colleague. She is always filled with supportive, inspired love and light but is not obviously extraordinary. Reading her story is magical, inspiring, and awakening because of this. It is a story of the extraordinary in the ordinary; a recounting of experiences we all may have had to some degree but lack understanding of, or it may be that we have allowed conditioning to lock us into a permanent disability or difficulty. Dawn has done her inner work both in this lifetime and previous ones. I say that because her innate ability to navigate through and use these difficult and sometimes traumatic situations could leave others feeling broken and bewildered. Yet it is remarkable that she came out the other side, shining. Dawn's bliss is in teaching others and in following her path. Her life has become a lesson on how to gracefully navigate the call to Spirit even when it calls in the loss of our very senses or our life! Reading her story and making new connections for myself enabled me to see some of my health difficulties from a whole new perspective.

Every life has a divine plan that unfolds like a flower and there is a purpose for every flower, every life. From the higher viewpoint that my work as an astrologer offers, I can see our lives are not random. Reading thousands of people's astrology charts (maps of the sky depicting when they take their first breath) has shown me that I can see a person's purpose, lessons, life events, work, and passions, all without knowing them intimately. Our soul has a unique journey and if we can elevate our point of view on life we begin to understand we are all here for a purpose and there are reasons for all the difficulties in our lives. All the seemingly random events lead us toward something specific. We are not victims of fate, nor are we random independent beings fighting for survival. We are on a journey from something to something much greater in our lives as Spirit. Though we are not meant to know everything through our minds, we can align with this higher perspective of our lives by embracing all aspects of ourselves, and the circumstances we find ourselves in. There is a deeper harmony to life beyond what our minds can fully grasp, and I believe we ultimately have what it takes to grow out of the fertile soil of our difficulties into something ever new and more conscious.

This story of Dawn's unique challenges and her way of using them to unveil her connection to Spirit and a higher and deeper understanding of her life journey can inspire a new attitude about our lives, possibly even helping us to see our struggles from a higher vantage point.

Michael Moon)O(

Astrologer, Composer, Musician, Artist
www.thetempleofsound.com

Prologue

This is not my home. This planet I reside on is not my home. I am just visiting. This body I reside in is not my home. I am just visiting. I am merely renting this vehicle in the form of this body to experience the physical, mental, and emotional aspects of human existence.

From 1968 to 2003, Dawn James only knew this home but within and around her something was stirring, restless, waiting patiently for the right time to show her where she really came from and what she truly was.

In 2003 I was presented with a choice: return home, leave this place, this life, this body, and everyone I knew and loved and return to Oneness, Nothingness, or remain. There you have it. I stood at that doorway for several moments though it felt like an eternity. I remembered what was on the other side: no beginning, no end, the state of bodiless consciousness, boundlessness, and true freedom. Was I to proceed and merge into Oneness, Nothingness, like the rivers that flow into the ocean to be seen no more?

There are many aspects of physical and spiritual existence that have been assigned different labels by different cultures. In 2003, I was given an opportunity to consciously realize my spirituality and experience many of these aspects of being spiritual. At times, these experiences were embodied within my physical form and sometimes without.

As I share these experiences with you, I realize that until recently I didn't have the full vocabulary to properly describe all that happened to me and what it has meant in my life. Not only that, but I was also still integrating the lessons into my life. In some ways, all the veils had not yet been lifted. It is as if we live our lives in a veil of illusion and this veil separates us from the reality of our innate powers and abilities. It separates us from the truth. We go through life and have experiences that bring us closer to or further from the truth that we are spiritual beings having a human experience, and it is up to each of us to go through, sit with, analyze, learn from, and integrate these experiences into our lives. I can do that for you because I kept a written account since the tender age of 38, in 2003, documenting every new experience I had in my waking hours as well as my dreams and visions. While I didn't always know what was happening to me or why, I am grateful that I had the foresight to document the events, sights, sounds, and even the smells in what became known as my "Spirit Journal," a journal that remains close to my bed even to this day.

The World We Live In

As I look back, this is what I have learned. We live our lives in a certain way and fall into a routine or a pattern of behaviour. Life becomes predictable to the point that we no longer think about our actions or reactions for that matter. We have said and thought and done the same things so many times that we become unconscious little humans existing on autopilot. Some of us find ourselves at a point in life, standing at the fork in the road, as these patterns we have created suddenly begin to look and feel unusual, uncomfortable, even foreign to us. Some of us begin to feel a stirring inside, a restlessness. There is a question that begins to echo over and over again in our heads. Is this all there is? We feel hungry but not for food. We feel that something is missing but cannot articulate what it is. Then the ultimate question erupts in our conscious minds... Why am I here? I heard this question echo for months in my mind leading up to my awakening, my liberation, and my ultimate freedom. Since then, I have come to learn that to only live as physical beings, is like living at 10% capacity. We are living limited lives. We are fragmented and incomplete. It matters not whether these limitations are self-imposed or simply imposed by societal dogma and man-made principles and codes for which we are led to believe we are forever bound. Either way, it has kept us from knowing ALL aspects of ourselves.

When we are born our bodies are pristine and shiny, like a new toy. We are in awe. Our physicality is a massive jigsaw puzzle that we need to configure, but this jigsaw puzzle box has no lid, no instructions, no preview images of what we are trying to accomplish here. We must figure it out on our own. Have you ever stopped to look at how babies evolve physically? They muster the effort to evolve from lying to sitting, from sitting to standing, and apply more effort still to evolve from standing to walking. And they never had to read any manual to accomplish this. Remarkable!

Many people do not realize the magnificence of what babies do and learn between birth and 18 months. The analogy is like progressing from making a fire by rubbing sticks together to building a rocket ship that is ignited by fuel, all within 18 months. I am fascinated by this progression. I am in awe of a baby's unspoken innate intelligence during that period. What happens to us after we become mobile little toddlers and man-made language is thrust down our throats? We are taught what the previous generation knows. We are told stories that the previous generation heard. We receive the rules, codes, and expectations that the previous generation was given; all hand-me-down stuff. And so, the cycle of limiting beliefs and inherited values begins again. More patterns to follow. It is a sad state, don't you think?

We walk into the library of physical life. The door is shut behind us and we begin to open the books before us, one at a time, and start believing that all knowledge must only come from these external sources. So, we study hard, memorize, regurgitate, and retell it to the *next* generation.

I have witnessed those who entered that library and are still there. I have also met those who chose to leave, and I see more and more people putting down the books and looking around… looking for a way out.

I had the pleasure of working for two self-made millionaires during my corporate career. Neither of them had a university degree, in fact, neither of them even finished elementary school. How is this possible you might ask? Well, these two had entered the library of physical life, opened a book or two, and said, "This is not for me." They found a window and crawled the hell out! Relying on their innate intelligence, gifts, and abilities, they became millionaires. Before my awakening, I was fortunate that both became mentors in my life. They were indeed living angels on my journey.

The truth is most people are going through life not fully awake and some are flat out sleepwalking. The good news is that anyone can wake up at any time, in childhood or adulthood. If we only pay attention to the bumps in the road of life, we may come to see that they are opportunities to expand ourselves and our view of existence.

After I woke up in 2003, I became a Conscious Observer of my life, including my past, present, and possible future. When I reflected on my past from infancy and started writing about my bumps in the road of life, something amazing began to unfold. I began to see a pattern in my timeline, something I had never paid attention to before. During my childhood and into my teens, I experienced some monumental events. What some may describe as traumatic events, I believe were tests. In the first phase of my life before becoming an adult I had been tested several times, pushed to a point of surrendering to something greater than myself, and each time something was revealed to me. This is my story of the lifting of veils, of revelations, and waking up to my life.

What Am I?

I am All that Is, expressed as a spiritual being that is currently on vacation as Dawn James.

Who Am I?

I am an Awakened One who chose to return.

Resilience

My life has been anything but easy. It has been filled with paradoxes, ironies, unexplained phenomenon, and many WTF moments. Some days I wonder how I have remained sane over the decades. In writing my life story, as I look back, I have come to realize that I have endured more than one 'death' – the death of my senses, my appetite, my life. As a result of these events, resilience became my middle name as I was forced to try to make sense of these experiences, or at least muster enough strength to withstand them. They say what does not kill you makes you stronger. Well, I am still here. Fasten your seat belt and get ready for a roller coaster ride into my life as Dawn James.

I was born just before sunset, yet they named me Dawn.

I consider myself an introvert, yet I made a very grand, almost diva-like, entrance into the world in 1965. This was the beginning of an endless chain of ironies and paradoxes.

A baby girl made history, twice, in a hospital in the Caribbean. She was the longest baby girl on record at 26½ inches, and she was the largest baby that year, hands down, weighing in at just shy of a whopping 12 pounds. Spoiler alert: I am an only child.

My parents became parents in their mid-thirties, not by design but by circumstance. Mom had tried for years to carry a baby to full term, and after the third miscarriage she found the courage to try again, and I arrived. It was a difficult labour for her, to say the least. You see, most babies in the last trimester begin to turn head down, in preparation for the birthing process. But for some unknown reason – maybe it was my Aries rising – I refused to turn head down and remained forward-facing and feet down (ouch). When I was much older, my dad would tell me stories about the weeks leading up to my birth and how the midwives and doctors attempted to turn my head down but nothing worked. Now that I am a mother and have delivered three babies all under 8½ pounds, I cannot imagine what my mom had to endure giving birth to a 26½ inch long, 12 pound, forward-facing, breach baby! God bless her, she survived.

My parents emigrated to Canada before I could even walk. Canada is where I have lived for almost my entire childhood and adult life. I am grateful they chose Canada because it gave our family a safe, peaceful place to live and the opportunity to thrive. My dad was a mechanical engineer. He could fix anything with a motor. He worked on boats, cars, trains, you name it. I think the only thing he did not tinker with was a rocket ship. He was my biggest cheerleader all through school. He told me to keep my chin up and put my best foot forward, always. Dad tended to be nomadic so our family moved quite a bit between Quebec and Ontario. I did not enjoy that, especially when I started school and began to make friends. I remember I had my first best friend in Grade One. The following year, my dad announced we were moving. I was so upset with him on the day we moved when I had to say goodbye to my best friend that I didn't speak to my dad for three weeks. The irony of refusing to speak to my dad would come back to haunt me as a teenager. They say karma is a B****.

My mom was a seamstress and had worked for herself since she was 21. She had amazing fashion design skills and her clientele often included many of Toronto's upper-class women. I didn't know it at the time, but as I became a teenager, I would recognize their names in the media. It was cool having rich and famous women come to our little, two-bedroom apartment in Toronto for fashion fittings. My mom was a humble, hardworking woman who taught me to hem and do intricate needlework. She also taught me how to be independent and self-reliant. We had many conversations about her life growing up in the islands, what it meant to be a woman and a lady (two different things), and life in general. Mom was also the anchor to my dad's ever-sailing boat. Dad was a big spender while Mom was the one who saved for a rainy day. I guess opposites do attract. However, the one trait that both my parents shared that I am grateful rubbed off on me, was resilience. They never let a difficult situation define or limit them. They recovered quickly, were very adaptable, and expected no less from me as you will learn.

Resilience would play a pivotal role in my life and I believe, wholeheartedly, that resilience kept me safe on my bumpy and often traumatic journey. For this, I will be ever grateful.

Time to Tell a New Tale

For almost two decades as I travelled and spoke around the world, I presented the 'fairy tale' version of my life, summed up in 150 words, and it went something like this:

"I grew up in Toronto, Ontario. Only child. I have loved music since forever and fell in love with the piano when I saw Liberace playing one day on TV when I was three. After begging my parents for five years, I eventually received a piano for my eighth birthday. Had my first recital at age nine and was with the Royal Conservatory for over a decade. But life got in the way as I went to university, started my career, met a guy, got married, and had three beautiful, healthy children.

In 2003, I had a profound experience that catapulted me into the world of spirituality. Quit my 72-hour per week toxic corporate gig and did some intense soul searching. I became a sound healer and writer. In 2010, my hubby and I became empty nesters. Now I am location-independent, doing what I love and loving what I do. I am a Lightworker."

The truth is that fairy tales do not exist, along with Santa Claus, the tooth fairy, and tax-free living. The jury is undecided on Bigfoot, aka Sasquatch.

It is time to get raw and real on the absolute roller-coaster, WTF journey I have experienced, and how extraordinary pivotal moments redefined my world with each unveiling.

The Vision

I believe this vision first occurred around age three and played over and over in my life for almost 50 years. I routinely travelled to this place in my dreams while my little body lay still on my bed, and found myself standing in front of the exact, same tree.

I like it here. I will stay awhile.

Look at the leaves on that tree. I have never seen leaves like that before. They play with the warm breeze, turning this way and that. It almost looks like a hand waving hello to me. My eyes roam upwards, higher than the tallest trees, and my attention is drawn to some fluffy white clouds, softly and slowly rolling by. I gaze at them until I begin to see shapes. I love imagining and seeing all those odd shapes, especially the funny animal shapes in the sky. The sun's rays kiss my cheeks. I smile. I stop daydreaming and my attention returns to the earth. Everything is a luscious shade of green. I return to tending to the animals. I am so excited as we just had a kid. I love baby goats. I pick up our new arrival. As I carry her to a bed of straw, I can feel her heartbeat and her warmth fills my heart with love.

I like it here. I will stay awhile.

Where is this place? Why do I keep landing here?

Hopscotch

"**M**orning Mama. Guess what? I played hopscotch last night."

"Dawny, you mean you played hopscotch yesterday with your friends."

"No Mama. Last night I played. I was making really big hops and I jumped so far on these big balls, but I never fell off."

"Dawny, you cannot jump onto a ball - balls are round. You are a silly Billy," Mom smiled and turned her attention from me to her skillet where she scrambled some eggs for our breakfast.

I was three years old. I would continue to play 'hopscotch' through the cosmos throughout my childhood. But how does a young girl articulate jumping from planet to planet, when she does not know what a planet is?

Five years later, our teacher gave us an assignment and it was my first recollection of having to stand up in front of the class to speak. My assignment was to share something about our solar system with the class.

Each day for a month, a different student would do their presentation. We could bring cue cards in case we forgot any facts or details. At age eight, I spoke for 30 minutes about our solar system. I explained the order of the planets from Mercury to Pluto. I also named all the moons of each planet, their relative distance from the sun, and the length of their orbits. I shared their relative distances from each other and what the planets were comprised of (i.e., gases, temperature, etc.). I spoke for 30 minutes, never looking at any cue cards. My teacher and classmates were shocked. I could have talked for another hour as the time seemed to speed by so quickly. I just took it as a matter of fact. I was sharing something I already knew.

I'm not certain whether my teacher shared my speech with my parents but if she had then maybe, just maybe, my mama would have believed me when I said five years earlier that I played hopscotch through the cosmos at night.

I honestly believe that young children remember or know where they really come from. Veils do not exist for them or are as thick as they are when we become adults, socialized into doctrines and dogmas.

Hopscotch

It is my personal belief that infants and young children can easily slip between physical and ethereal states of being because their fontanelles are still soft and pliable. My spiritual experiences and teachings have affirmed this. The fontanelle represents soft membrane gaps between the cranial bones at the top of the head. It is exceptionally soft in infants and hardens as we become older. One interesting thing about the fontanelle is that it has a pulse that echoes that of our heartbeat, like synchronistic resonance. The fontanelle can act as a doorway for our Spirit/Consciousness to exit and enter. When my children were infants, I observed how they would fall asleep, how they slept, and how they woke up. In time, I observed changes in their eye movements, their breathing patterns, and even their facial expressions, and could tell when they were in their physical body and when they were out. There is so much wisdom and wonder in babies. Yet in the absence of mature vocabulary, the antics of children are usually shrugged off with 'you have an active imagination' or 'you had a bad dream.'

I stopped telling Mama about my nighttime adventures and kept them to myself. As I grew older, my 'hopscotch' episodes would diminish but they never truly stopped.

CHAPTER ONE

Activated (Age 7)

Silence Unveils Empathy

Like every other day, I woke up and got ready for school. I didn't know what time it was, but the house was unusually quiet. I wondered if they were still sleeping. I walked to my parents' room and opened the door. They weren't there. Nature was calling so I popped into the bathroom. When I returned to the hallway the mystery was solved. Yup, they were awake and in the kitchen. My nose knows the smell of a heavenly breakfast. I inhaled. Something yummy was being cooked. Oh, the smell of breakfast was so rich that day! I could almost taste the salt on the bacon. I smelled that delicious flavour that only homemade bread has, with melted butter and…was that…cheddar cheese? Yes, cheddar cheese was slowly melting on top. The nose knows. I got dressed, brushed my teeth, then quickly ran down the stairs to greet that feast in the kitchen.

I opened my mouth to say, "Morning." I saw Mom's lips moving but I didn't hear her. Dad turned to look at me and I also saw his lips moving but I heard nothing. I suddenly gasped for air and felt weak in my legs. I had never experienced a panic attack before but clearly, I was not OK. Mom saw the look of panic on my face and walked up to me. She looked into my eyes and gently placed her hands on my shoulder. The loving look in her eyes calmed the storm in my head. Mom had a gift for taking the mountain of an unplanned event and shrinking it to the size of a molehill in minutes. I think it was one of her superpowers. Her lips moved again but I didn't know what she was trying to say to me. *"Breathe Dawn. Take a deep breath.* Look at me. Everything will be OK."

Intensely, I watched her lips to try to get some sense of what she was saying. I barely managed to recognize the word OK. She raised her right hand and pointed to her ear and her lips formed the words, "Can you hear me?" I shook my head from left to right to gesture no. *No, I cannot hear you! I cannot hear anything! What is happening to me? Why is this happening to me?*

My dad sat there in disbelief that his little girl might be deaf. How did this happen? Why did this happen? Only God knows. A minute later Dad stood up, walked over to me, and placed his palm on my forehead as if to check my temperature to see if I had a fever. No fever. Then he ran down to the basement and returned to the kitchen with two things. He had a phone book (yup, they were still around in the 70s) and a whistle. While looking at me, he slammed the phone book on the kitchen table. Nothing! Again, I shook my head from left to right to gesture no. He then picked up a whistle and blew into it and the same result occurred. I shook my head no. Dad started pacing and the storm in my head returned as I watched him walk up and down the hallway.

I was seven years old and I had woken up deaf!

The rest of that day was a blur to me, although I vividly recall getting on the school bus at some point. You see, no matter what was going on in my life, no matter how sick I may have been feeling, from kindergarten to university, I never missed a school day (except when I got chicken pox). I must have written a note that morning begging my parents to let me on the school bus because there I was, sitting on that yellow bus with my classmates. By the time I had eaten that heavenly breakfast my nerves had calmed down.

Reflecting on my childhood, I was never the kind of person to get hysterical or freak out, at least no major freaking out that anyone would ever see. I tended to keep things to myself, so while there might have been a storm raging in my head as my heart beat a little too fast and my blood pressure steadily rose, to my friends and family I was cool as a cucumber on the outside. Sometimes this trait served me well and sometimes it had major health ramifications, and eventually, it took a toll on my body. It may have been attributed to being an only child as I was very mature for my age and was always around adults who were calm and collected. Perhaps it was a learned behaviour, I don't know. All I do know is that I accepted that this was how it would be, and I convinced my parents to let me go to school. My mom wrote a note for me to give to my teacher, explaining that I wouldn't be participating in any class discussions and to call her if I felt uncomfortable and needed to leave school early. She also wrote to inform them of the situation and that I had a doctor's appointment the following day and would be away from school. Her PS read, "Dawn insisted on not missing a day of school."

Insights

I sat on the bus and it felt like the first time I had seen those children. It was an odd feeling as if it was my first day at school and I didn't know anyone on the bus. Yet I remember smiling as I sat there in silence just observing everyone. This was my first experience with being an Observer, and even though I wasn't interacting with anyone, I felt very connected to everyone at the same time. It was a new and strange feeling for me. I thought, *when your world is silent you see so much more.* I paid close attention to facial expressions, hand gestures, who was making faces, who was laughing, who was staring out the window, daydreaming. One or two kids were hurriedly writing in their notebooks to finish homework they didn't get done the night before. Some were feeling sad because they wanted to be at home.

Feeling...sad...feeling. Feeling sad?! I looked at a little girl with wavy strawberry blonde hair wearing a blue bomber jacket. She sat by herself looking out the window at nothing in particular.

As I watched her, I felt that she was feeling sad. I began to feel sad. Why am I sad? No, wait. Hold on. No, no I wasn't sad. I was not sad. I *felt* her sadness. Ah, OK? Maybe I needed to look elsewhere on that school bus. I decided to look at our bus driver. He was always so calm and polite to all the kids. I often wondered how he could concentrate on driving with so many kids chitter-chattering. I typically sat near the front door of the bus to make a quick exit, so I had more time to play before the bell rang. *Good logic for a seven-year-old, right?* I might have been five feet away from the driver. I tried not to stare as I moved my eyes from the top of his head to his feet. I guess you could say I was scanning him. What I was looking for? I am not sure to this day. I just couldn't help it. After a few moments, I felt my heartbeat slowing down, just a little. *Breathe slowly. Deep inhale, deep exhale.* My breathing slowed considerably and that is when I felt it. *Observe. Connect.*

Somewhere between his ears and his chin, I felt an achy feeling, a low numbing pain. I touched my right ear. No, no, I was fine, I had no pain there. It wasn't mine but I felt the pain in his jaw as if it was in my jaw. Wow, that was freaky! I was in awe but I quickly reminded myself that it wasn't mine. I looked back at the other kids on the bus. There were about 20 kids on the bus that day and thank goodness it was a short ride. I tried not to look at anyone else for too long. I think I'd had enough of LOOK and FEEL for one day.

When the bus finally stopped at our school, I stood up. I couldn't help myself; I had to say something to the driver as I felt sad that he was in that much pain. How could I talk to him though when I couldn't hear a thing? I quickly grabbed a pencil from my backpack, tore out part of a page from my notebook, and wrote him a note. I walked up to him slowly, smiling as I placed the note in his hands. Then I turned and quickly ran out before he could read it. The note said, "Don't chew gum so much because it is giving you pain in your jaw."

It is said many times that when we lose one of our senses, the other senses become stronger.

The day that my sense of hearing stopped working was the day I became aware that I could feel the world around me in a different way. I had never felt that kind of connection to anyone before. At first, it freaked me out, and I couldn't tell if it was me or them, but in time I began to discern what I felt like with more clarity. This day had brought me the gift or remembrance of being empathic. I had been 'tested,' no doubt. God knew why. Looking back to that incident in 1972, many may regard this as a traumatic experience, but I didn't receive it that way. I did not allow fear to enter my being. I recognized that I was given an opportunity to experience other senses and a new way of being in this world. I regarded this experience as a gift.

I remember my parents accompanying me to the doctor's office. I had to have several hearing tests. They were puzzled as the doctor did not have an explanation. The next morning, my hearing returned, as mysteriously as it had disappeared two days earlier. I would never be the same again. My empathic abilities were now activated.

Reflections

There are different types of empaths. What they all share, however, is the ability to deeply connect to information from another source. What differs is the source and how or where it is processed in their body. For example, an empath may connect to the energetic or emotional information from other people, plants, animals, even the planet. Some empaths will feel with their aura, have visions, or energy may stir in their hands or feet. They may have a gut feeling or a picture appears in their third eye, or they see a 'sign' or may even receive a message that only they can hear.

As a young child, my empathy was expressed in one of two ways: psychometry and clairalience.

Psychometry: The first time I ever saw my dad cry was when I was about eight years old. We were living in a two-bedroom apartment and in the living room, there was a floor-to-ceiling shelving unit. You know, the ones where you place the TV, but you have other shelves around it to place books, knickknacks, and the like. On the bottom shelf of the TV shelving unit were the family albums. Every now and then, I would look at the photos in the album, and every year I loved slipping my birthday party photos in the little plastic slots, remembering the fun I had at my party. One afternoon as I was flipping through the album, I came across a photo of a young Black woman. She may have been in her late teens or early twenties. I remember looking at her facial features and her eyes and they looked vaguely familiar to me, but what got my attention was the sadness I felt while looking into her eyes. I slipped into her soul through gazing at her eyes, like dipping into a pool of cool water on a hot summer's day. A feeling of sadness engulfed me like a heavy wet blanket. There was so much pain wrapped up in that sadness and I just sat with it all. My dad walked by a minute or two later and asked what I was doing sitting on the floor. I showed him the picture of the young woman and I explained that she was very sad. I went on to tell him that she was very sad when she died, and she was alone. She was a kind person and very smart. I felt sad for her how she…

I looked up to see tears running down my dad's cheeks as his eyes just stared into space while hanging onto my every word. "Daddy? Are you OK?" As I was about to stand up, my mom came into the living room as my dad turned and walked past her. She watched him as he closed the bedroom door. Mom suddenly turned to me and saw the album lying open on the floor. She asked me what happened and I repeated what I told my dad. She took one look at the photo and warned me not to talk about things like that again! She hurriedly picked up the album and placed it on the top shelf, far out of my reach at that age. What did I do wrong? I was only talking about what I felt and saw. There would be countless other times as a child I would innocently start talking about what I saw and felt in photos, when walking into a room, feeling the people on the public transit, and time and time again my mom would tell me, "Stop talking about things like that…stop talking period." After hearing her comments dozens of times and seeing that disapproving look on her face, I simply and eventually stopped talking.

When I got older it became a novelty. Some of my girlfriends knew about my ability to 'read' photos. I went from feeling like a freak of nature from my mother's response to being 'unique' with a 'cool gift' to a handful of friends. It came in handy when my girlfriends would show me pictures of their suitors and potential boyfriends and ask for a 'reading' on them. *"Dawn what do you think? Is he a nice guy? Will he be faithful to me? Do you sense any skeletons in his closet?"*

When I became a mom and my children were preteens and brought home their school class pictures, I loved to scan their class photos and would identify which kids were the class clowns, which ones were the bullies, the loners, the stoners, and so on. They would ask me, *"How do you know that? You haven't even met them."* or *"Yes he is, or she is, but how did you know that?"* I shrugged it off as a lucky guess.

I wasn't ready to tell my kids that it was a natural gift of deep empathy. My mother conditioned me very well not to tell others about my gifts. But when I saw my dad crying when I was a little girl 'reading' the lady's photo in the album, I could not let that go. Somehow, I had hurt him, and I needed to understand why I made him cry. Whenever I asked my mother why Dad was crying, she would dismiss my question with, "You are too young to understand." Several years would pass before my mother felt I was old enough to understand and she could explain who the lady was in the photo. My dad's youngest sister was murdered by her fiancé. She was an exceedingly kind person and an excellent student who was studying to be a schoolteacher. And there I was, a little girl of eight, telling my dad how sad this lady was when she died. I was slowly beginning to understand that even a photo had information that someone could access if they knew how. This fascinated me!

Clairalience: The second empathic ability I chose/choose not to use since childhood. I didn't recognize it as an ability until I was in my early 30s and was watching a program about certain dogs that were trained to smell people with cancer. Yes, cancer! I was fascinated by the program as they explained this uncanny canine ability. Dogs have an incredibly sensitive sense of smell that can detect the odour signatures of various types of cancer. Among others, they can detect colon cancer, prostate cancer, breast cancer, and melanoma by sniffing people's skin, bodily fluids, or breath. Incredible.

When I was a young child, and my dad drove the family car to work, Mom and I would often travel on public transit, either by bus or subway. One time we were living in Montreal, and we had to take the subway to get to the Mega Mall. I was sitting beside my mom and as kids often do, I never really paid attention to where we were going or what the subway stop name was. When Mom stood up, I stood up. She would always hold my hand when the train doors opened for us to walk out together. This time when Mom stood up and I stood up, a large woman brushed by me to get the vacant seat. To this day, I remember what she looked like: pale skin, auburn-coloured hair, wearing a dark purple winter coat. She had a serious look on her face. I happened to inhale as she brushed by me. I immediately felt uncomfortable. I sensed she had been fighting, perhaps an argument with her husband, and her anger was still raging inside her. I felt her anger but quickly shook it off. I turned my head from gazing at the woman in the purple coat only to see my mom standing on the platform and the doors were closing with me still inside the train. "Mom!" I shouted. My mother looked horrified as the train was about to move. She banged on the window and I saw her put up her index finger. My heart was racing inside but luckily my mind was moving at a steady pace and I was still thinking. I guessed that Mom was telling me the number one or next stop when she held up her index finger. That was the first time I was alone on the subway. I was scared. What if she couldn't find me? How would I get home? What if I never saw her again? *Dawn stop. Get off at the next stop.* As soon as the train stopped, I walked off and ran over to the wall. I planted my back on the wall like it was stuck with crazy glue so the adults walking by would not accidentally push me around. I waited there for what felt like hours. *Please, Mom… find me. Please.* A few minutes went by when the next train came to the same stop. I watched, I waited, I watched. There were so many people, how would she see me? When that train pulled off it got much quieter and there she was, a few feet away, smiling. She gave me the biggest hug I can ever remember. We proceeded with our outing to a nearby mall to shop for a baby shower. I loved riding the escalators in the mall; it almost felt like one of the rides at Man and His World (former Montreal Expo grounds). I was standing one step in front of Mom on the escalator when two people, a man, and a woman, walked past us. I caught a whiff of one of them and I started getting information and a moving image like a movie playing. I didn't like what I saw: a man intertwined with a woman. It looked gross. I shook my head quickly and remembered where I was. I quickly grabbed Mom's hand and we stepped off the escalator together. We finally arrived in the baby clothes section. Mom was busy looking for something yellow or green because we didn't know if it would be a boy or girl. I could see the store clerk walking towards us and as she got close to me, I held my breath and stepped away from her. She probably thought I was shy. I exhaled. Nothing. Thank goodness, I thought, and I resumed breathing normally.

Mission accomplished! Mom bought a baby outfit. We did some other shopping and then returned to the escalator.

From that day on, whenever anyone was walking past me, I would hold my breath, until it became a reflex action. It was very tricky whenever I got into an elevator. Often I would wait until an elevator came with no one in it or no one standing with me to get on it. To this day, I dislike going into crowded places or social events where I am near others. And there I was watching a show about dogs detecting cancer cells in humans using smell. That was one gift I did not want to have or use. I just didn't want to know or see or get information in that way, so I consciously chose to keep that gift dormant.

It is not easy being empathic. You feel too much. You can get overwhelmed receiving information, especially information you did not request. And once you get it, what do you do with it? Who do you share it with? I felt compelled to write a note to our school bus driver because I knew he was in a lot of pain. However, growing up, I mainly kept that unsolicited information to myself because I didn't want others to feel uncomfortable around me.

CHAPTER TWO

I Don't Want (You) to Go (Age 8)

Loss of Speech Unveils Speaking My Truth

The year I turned eight, two amazingly delightful events happened along with another unveiling. The first and most delightful thing was meeting my paternal grandmother for the first time (other than when I was born, I am told). I was so excited she was coming to visit us that I couldn't sleep, the night before. I woke up super early, put on my Sunday best dress, and Mom, Dad and I drove to the airport to meet her. Granny was not only coming to visit us, but she would be spending the entire summer at our place. Christmas in July! I remember holding

Mom's hand at the airport, standing near an escalator. Dozens of people were walking quickly past us carrying suitcases. Then I felt it, an unexplainable magnetic pull. I just knew she was close by. I looked as far as I could, and I remember seeing a pair of feet wearing brown leather shoes step onto the escalator. I pulled free from my mother's grasp and started running towards the escalator to meet those feet.

"Dawn, come back here!" Mom yelled. (Remember the subway incident the year before.)

"She's here!" I shouted.

I must have looked like a football player weaving in and out of everyone, running towards the escalator. I saw the legs, the skirt, then I looked up at the face. "Granny!!!" I shouted. She started to laugh and opened her arms and gave me a ginormous granny hug. I was beaming from ear to ear. We descended together to meet Mom and Dad at the foot of the escalator. Mom did not look pleased that I had left her side to chase a pair of feet but it didn't matter… they were the right feet.

We had moved back to Ontario by then and were living in a two-bedroom apartment in Toronto. Granny stayed in my room that summer and each morning she had the same ritual. She would wake up ever so quietly and reach for her Bible. I swear she prayed for about two hours every morning. Why is it that adults seem to take so long to do something when you are a child?

I still vividly remember all the moments we spent together. Granny taught me how to crochet and do needlepoint. We spent countless hours together with coloured thread creating all sorts of designs and learning different stitching patterns. To this day, I still have a little pink apron with a beautiful flower design tucked away that I made with her that summer. She was a gentle soft-spoken woman, and oh the stories she could tell – especially about raising four boys in the Caribbean. My dad and his brothers were quite a handful and had many adventures growing up.

Then the big day came. There was a knock at the door. I looked outside and saw a moving truck. Oh no, were we moving again? No way! We didn't have anything packed. What gives? A man spoke to my dad at the door. Dad nodded his head and five minutes later, two men wheeled in a beautiful upright piano into our little apartment. They gently placed it in the living room. Pinch me, I am dreaming. Oh, happy day! My wish had come true after five years of asking to have a piano of my own to play.

When I was a toddler, one of the first toys I picked out at the store was a little blue toy piano with multi-coloured keys. I took that toy piano everywhere we went – on the bus, to the grocery store, the library, the dentist's office – everywhere. At one point, I think I had about four toy pianos in my bedroom. I just couldn't have enough. That day my wish came true and I finally got a real piano. On the front of the piano were the words Mason and Risch. I didn't care if it said Tom and Jerry because it was mine!

It was an early birthday present, as my birthday was in the fall, but they timed it to be delivered when Granny was visiting. I think the biggest surprise I received that summer, even bigger than the piano, was waking up the next morning and hearing a beautiful melody from the living room. I raised my head from the pillow and rubbed my eyes. Where was she? I sat up and listened to the sound of the keys and the recurring beat. 1-2-3, 1-2-3, 1-2-3. It was a waltz! I ran to the living room and there she was sitting at the piano, playing. Granny could play the piano? I scooted over to sit with her and was in awe as she played. Time stood still that morning as I watched her hands stroke the keys ever so gently to a beautiful melody.

My first piano teacher was my granny. She taught me to play the song, You're in My Heart (*Du, du, liegst mir im Herzen*), a German folk song and waltz. Granny didn't read music and that made the fact that she taught me how to play even more special. We were inseparable that summer as we went everywhere together. I felt like I had a sister, best friend, mother, and granny all rolled into one beautiful package.

At the end of August, it was time to say goodbye. On the day she left, I felt a deep sadness that I couldn't explain. My body ached all over and my chest felt heavy. I was more than sad to see her go. I felt like I would never see Granny again. The morning after she left, I woke up with a sore throat. As the day went on the soreness grew worse, until I found it difficult to swallow my saliva, let alone solid food. By dinner time, I was barely able to speak. It was too hard to even try so I stopped talking. I couldn't talk for a few days. Sore throats, dry coughs, and laryngitis would come to plague me throughout my childhood and adult life.

Insights: Throat Chakra

The throat chakra is connected to the way you express your life with utmost authenticity. It is about communicating your thoughts, feelings, and intentions, clearly and accurately. The throat chakra, also known as the Vishuddha, is the place where we work on expanding our voice and the power of will.

Some physical symptoms of blockage in the throat chakra which I experienced were:

- chronic sore throat
- hoarseness
- hyper and hypothyroid issues
- laryngitis
- temporomandibular disorders of the jaw (commonly known as TMJ)

Non-physical signs of blockage that I had to deal with during my youth were:

- fear of speaking
- inability to express thoughts
- shyness

Reflections

There is a vast difference between losing one's voice and choosing not to speak. There were times in my life when I chose not to speak, like when my dad decided we were moving when I was in Grade One and I gave him the silent treatment for three weeks.

However, when I look at moments in my life when I *lost* my voice, I noticed a pattern.

At age eight, I got laryngitis when my granny left our place. I never saw her again. I got a phone call one day from my dad telling me she had died. I was 21 years old. I cried for three days, virtually non-stop. My chest felt like a piano was sitting on it and I lost my voice for a week while I experienced the intense emotional pain of losing her.

On the eve of my 13th birthday, my parents sat me down and said they were separating. They gave me 24 hours to tell them which parent I wanted to live with. Yup, 24 hours to decide. When my dad left town, I got a sore throat. A few days later I started to cough. It was a dry cough that would last almost eight months. I came to think of it as a cough from hell. It was so severe that I had to have chest x-rays which revealed I was developing scar tissue from coughing too hard.

As a teenager, my first heartbreak somehow triggered my thyroid to go into overdrive and I lost quite a bit of weight in a few short months.

As an empty nester, I was excited to be moving to a country with a much warmer climate to start a new life with my hubby. However, the thought of not seeing my friends, my three adult children, or my grandbaby for months on end was not a welcome one. It was a bittersweet time in my life. But 'Miss *appears to be* cool as a cucumber' was at it again. I busied myself packing, purging, decluttering, and getting ready for the big move. About three months before we were scheduled to leave, I started coughing. The dry cough grew noticeably more uncomfortable with each passing day and I had problems speaking. I felt exhausted only a few hours after I woke up in the morning. I was usually a high energy person, on the go from morning until late at night. It was clear something was off. When I started to breathe like I was gasping for air, I became genuinely concerned and drove myself to the hospital. Luckily, we lived in a small town and I was able to see the emergency room doctor in less than an hour. He asked me the usual questions, did the stethoscope test, and told me I would need to get x-rays.

"Why?" I asked.

He replied, "I just need to be sure."

Sure, of what? I thought.

Anyway, I reluctantly complied, had the x-rays, and waited longer for the results than my wait to see him when I arrived. He explained that I had walking pneumonia and I would need to rest for three weeks with no talking. I sat there in disbelief. He further explained that the pneumonia was the reason I was feeling tired. He also explained that although I could speak, I was straining my vocal cords and needed to be silent or my chords would get worse or damaged.

Did I listen to the doctor?

Well, not exactly. The first thing I did when I got home was to call my best friend to tell her about pneumonia and vocal strain. Her reply to me was, "I'm actually not surprised. Dawn, you are about to leave Canada; you are leaving friends and family behind. You are grieving and you are in denial that you are grieving, and to top things off I bet you haven't talked to anyone about what you are feeling, not even your husband."

Damn, she was spot on. *Did I mention my best friend is also a Reiki Master and EFT (emotional freedom technique) practitioner and is empathic?*

"Ok, I am listening. Tell me."

"Honey, your grief has turned inwards and is affecting your lungs and throat. Grief is the emotion of the lungs. If you are sad, say it, if you are going to miss your friends, say it out loud. Tell them, I am going to miss you big time. I love you."

I started to sob, "I am going to miss you too," and then a tsunami of tears came barreling down my cheeks. She did some distant Reiki for a few minutes. The tears subsided. "Thanks for listening, love you too," I said.

What I have come to learn from these periods of losing my voice due to energetic (blocked throat chakra) or emotional reasons (grief, loss, major change), is that I cannot continue to ignore my emotional body. We are sentient beings designed to feel. Isn't that one of the reasons we came here on *vacation* – to have mental, emotional, and physical experiences?

Each time I chose not to feel anything or suppressed my true feelings, they erupted into a physical issue. Ironically, by not expressing myself, my truth, how I was feeling, I lost the ability to express myself vocally. Ah, the irony of life.

How does an eight-year-old tell her parents she knows she will never see her granny alive again?

How does a 13-year-old come to terms with choosing which parent to live with while her heart is aching as she watches her parents split up? I loved them both and I knew that by choosing one, I was hurting the other. How do you talk about that and with whom? I had no siblings and no close friends to confide in. It felt more like a business decision, not an emotional one that day, but I was grieving for months, no years after my dad left. I don't regret my decision to live with my mom, but I do regret not having him in my life during my teen years.

Maybe this learned behaviour began with my relationship with my mother. I was continually told not to speak to anyone about what I saw or felt as an empath. When you are little and implicitly trust your parents, you comply. I internalized her disapproval of my abilities and began to suppress them.

By ignoring my emotions and not expressing what I was feeling, I created dissonance in my emotional body. I was not living in harmony with my head and heart, and my throat was in the middle of the battlefield. Spirit would repeat this lesson in my life again and again until I learned how to speak my truth without apology, guilt, or permission.

CHAPTER THREE

More Than Music Lessons (Age 9)

Loss of Sight Unveils Inner Confidence

Do you remember the bright new shiny piano I received at age eight? Unbeknownst to me, that little piano would be the key to opening many doors in my life and helped to shape the person I am today.

When you are a little child you don't know about this thing called 'status' in society. I know we lived in apartment buildings my entire childhood, we had one car, and we had food in the fridge. However, our family was not rich or barely considered middle-class. I remember Mom loved to go to her Bingo games with my godmother a few times a week. It was like a girl's night out for her. Once in a while, she won a few dollars here and there but one day in June, before my granny arrived, she won $2,500 at a Bingo game – her biggest winning ever – and the first thing she did was buy me a piano. I am eternally grateful for this gift because it became so much more than a pastime for me. I played the piano for hours at a time…it soothed my soul. I played when I felt sad and when I was happy. It was the first place I went when I got home from school.

Playing the piano also allowed me to use my left hand and that was important to me. Why? Because I was born left-handed; that was my natural state. Unfortunately, due to my mother's religious upbringing and beliefs, being left-handed was not natural in *her world*. By the time I started to pick up a fork or spoon or reached for a glass of water with my left hand, my mom quickly intervened and placed the object in my right hand. Our interpersonal battle began, ever so subtly. At one point, she took the stronghold position and started covering my left hand with a brown paper bag and tied it with twine. Let me tell you, that paper bag was on my left hand for hours at a time. I can still see the markings on my left wrist today from the twine that was bound around it. Eventually, I began using my right hand and by the time I started school I was a full-fledged converted right-handed person. Mother's mission was accomplished or so she thought.

Fortunately, my imprisonment came to an end when that piano arrived. For the first time in my life, I was free to use my left hand, without judgment or punishment. I felt free and empowered. Playing piano also opened new doors for me and helped me become a confident young woman, but my early days of lessons and recitals, especially piano recitals, were rough.

On my ninth birthday, Dad surprised me when we drove to a house and I was greeted by a lady named Mrs. Stevens. My dad announced that Mrs. Stevens was going to be my piano teacher. I was on cloud nine and gave him a gigantic hug. I smiled from ear to ear as I followed Mrs. Stevens into her music room. She was a loving but firm teacher. She challenged me to listen with intention and to recognize the notes on the keyboard. Not one note, but every note. We often played a game where I would stand a few feet away with my back facing the piano. Mrs. Stevens would play a note and then ask me to come up and play the same note. Yup, at age nine. At first, she would show me which scale she was picking a note from. There are a possible 12 notes that can be played on one scale (seven white keys, five black keys). Once I got the hang of that, she would expand it to two scales, then three scales, and so on. That game sharpened my listening skills and innate ability to find the exact key that she had played. Those skills would serve me well in a few months.

One afternoon, Mrs. Stevens handed me a flyer and said, "You are ready for your first recital." I was excited and a little nervous and asked her to explain what I had to do to prepare. She told me I had to practice a musical piece that I wanted to play. I had to practice it until I didn't need to read the notes to play it. Just play. It took me about eight weeks to get ready for my first recital. My parents were extremely excited as well. Mom made me a new dress just for the occasion; a beautiful light blue dress with princess sleeves, the first of many recital dresses to come.

The big day had arrived. I had six months of formal piano lessons, and I was about to perform my first piano recital at a nearby university. It looked like a little town to me with dozens of buildings and endless roads circling the campus. We parked near the building where the recital was taking place. We found the lecture hall and opened the unbelievably tall wooden doors. Oh my gosh, the room was huge, bigger than any room I had ever seen on TV. My eyes quickly darted across the seats and there she was. Mrs. Stevens smiled and waved at me. My parents and I sat beside her near the entrance doors to the lecture hall. She pointed to the stage where the piano was. That stage seemed so far away. How was I going to get down there? She then pointed to the three judges in attendance. I wasn't too concerned about them, however, I was very concerned about how many steps there were to walk down to the stage and then across the stage to the piano.

I patiently waited my turn until I heard them call my name and the name of the musical piece I was going to play. I stood at the top of the stairs. Perhaps I stood there a little too long, as everyone turned to watch me. They were waiting. Dozens of eyeballs looking at me felt like darts piercing my skin. *Please stop looking at me. Please stop.* I froze. My legs felt cold and stiff, like icicles. Oh my God, I wished the earth would open and I could fall in and disappear. I couldn't move! I felt so uncomfortable seeing so many eyes looking my way. I managed to slide my left foot forward onto the first step and then stepped down. Then I slid my right foot forward to step down. The people watching me must have thought I had just learned how to walk. *OK, two steps are done, with 16 more to go.* But with each step forward towards the stage, I could see from the side of the room that things were getting darker. It looked like someone was closing a black curtain from the sides of the lecture hall towards my direction. I felt a queasy feeling in my stomach and my forehead got warm. *This is no time to be sick, Dawn. Do not throw up. Focus.* I decided to walk a little faster. I needed to get to the stage before it got any darker. Those black curtains were moving in on me, across my eyes, and I could see less and less of the room. By the time I made it down those 18 steps and finally got to the stage, the black curtains had caught up to me, and all I could see was a tiny sliver of the piano seat. *Hurry up!* I quickly walked across the stage and abruptly sat down. *Oh my God! What is going on? And why today, of all days?* My heart raced and my head was very warm. Everything was black. I mean everything. No light, nothing but pitch black all around me. I could not see anything! *Breathe Dawn, breathe. Inhale slowly. Exhale slowly. Remember you do not need them.* Then I heard one of the judges say, "You may begin."

I focused all my energy on my teachings from Mrs. Stevens. I took a deep breath and gently placed my two thumbs on middle C on the keyboard. I envisioned the notes in my mind's eye. I took another deep breath and my fingers started moving across the keys. I melted into the sound. I poured my heart, mind, and soul into every note I played. I performed the piece exactly as I had practised it. The right notes, the right tempo. Once my fingers were in rhythm and my heart was calm, everything flowed with ease. I started to feel better. I was relieved that I couldn't see anyone and could just be one with the piano. Until I finished playing and found myself sitting there… once more, in the dark. Now what? There was no way I could find my way off the stage and walk up 18 steps to my parents. No way. The room was so eerily silent that you could hear a pin drop. I quickly raised my right hand and gestured, come here. The first person to rush to my side was my mom. I could smell her Lily of the Valley perfume that she always wore, even before she arrived at my side.

In a calm voice, she leaned over and asked me, "What is the matter"?

I told her, "I cannot see anything."

She said in her typical calm tone, "Take my arm."

I wrapped my arm around hers like a scarf wrapped around a neck. I was not letting go of her. She gently guided me to the end of the stage and helped me walk up the stairs to where my dad and piano teacher were sitting. At that moment, I was so thankful that I couldn't see anyone. It was bad enough trying to figure out what had just happened. To this day, I do not remember what was said between my piano teacher and my parents in that lecture hall. All I remember is asking them if we could leave the room as I was feeling like I couldn't breathe and my head was still warm. I desperately needed fresh air.

Mrs. Stevens, my parents, and I walked to the parking lot. I vaguely recall Mrs. Stevens said, "Perhaps it's my fault that she got very nervous." For some reason, she blamed herself for my intense nervousness. After that first recital, Mrs. Stevens would choose not to attend another, except for one more, in fear I would be nervous again. As soon as my parents and I got inside the car, I reached for the side of the door and felt the plastic handle. I quickly turned that handle to open the window and let the breeze blow on my face as we drove away. I pushed my head out the window like a giraffe reaching for tall trees. I needed to cool my head down as it felt like an oven. Within a few minutes of that welcome breeze, I began to see a sliver of light as the black curtains started to open very slowly until more light appeared and I was able to see my hands, my blue dress, the car seat, my parents sitting in the front seat, and the road. *What just happened and why?* I reached out toward the front seat and gently placed my hand on my mom's left shoulder. She looked into my eyes. No words were spoken. We didn't need to speak. She knew I would be OK. Three months later I had my second piano recital. I had practised hard and was ready for the challenge. However, unlike my first recital, that morning as I was getting dressed, wearing yet another new dress Mom had sewn for me, the black curtains returned from the sides of my eyes ... and I watched them move.

"MOM, it's happening again!" I shouted.

In a heartbeat, Mom rushed to my side. "What is happening?" she asked.

"Mom, the room is getting dark again and my head feels hot."

I started paying closer attention to how my body was changing just before it happened. My head, the sides, and the top of my head would get hot, and I felt queasy like just before you want to throw up.

Mom instructed me to sit down on the bed while she went to the kitchen to get me a glass of cold water. By the time she returned to my room, the black curtains were completely closed. The cold water helped my head feel a little better, but I couldn't see a thing.

"Dawn, what do you want to do?" she asked.

"I want to go to the recital," I replied.

Yes, at age nine, my mom asked me what *I wanted* to do. Since I was a toddler, my parents asked me to make choices and decisions. At first, it was which colour socks do you want to wear? What do you want for lunch? By the time I turned 12, the question was which parent do you want to live with? I had been groomed to think for myself from a young age. I was also trained to know that every choice has a cost or consequence. At that moment, I fully understood that I had two choices: to give up and not attend the recital, or to push ahead and finish what I was prepared to do. Quitting was not in my vocabulary.

Dad wasn't home that day so Mom and I had to take public transit. Once again, she gave me her arm as we left the house and rode the bus to my second recital. While I wasn't able to see for the entire ride, or during my performance, to my surprise once I finished playing the last note, my vision returned. I got up, walked across the stage, and returned to my seat beside Mom. *Relieved? Oh yes.* I remember watching my mother clasp her hands together like she was about to pray when she saw me walk upstairs by myself. She, too, was relieved that my sight had returned. Over the next nine years, I continued to play and perform. I formally studied music with the Royal Conservatory, both practical and theoretical. I enjoyed every moment of it. I had wonderful memories of taking road trips with my parents, staying in fancy hotels, and wearing new dresses at virtually every recital. I won many awards and trophies.

I also remember how grateful I was for my mom's arm to support and guide me, for you see, more often than not when I had a recital, I played the piano without any vision. We later learned that my temporary vision loss was somehow connected to my nervousness and shyness. Over the next few years, however, my nervousness would gradually diminish as I gained more confidence in entering and exiting rooms with dozens of people. I also gained more confidence in my abilities as a musician. I discovered that I didn't need my physical eyes to see the notes, nor did I need to see the people in the room to connect with them through sound. The confidence I gained by performing integrated into my academic studies. During these years of playing the piano, I also excelled in school, as I skipped three grades between age nine and 16, but more about that a little later.

I continued to play until life as an adult got in the way of my love of the piano. Just before my university graduation at age 19, I decided to close that chapter of my life. And guess who attended my last piano recital? Mrs. Stevens. I was so glad to see her. What a beautiful end to a melodic period in my life. After that final recital, I never again experienced another episode of temporary vision loss.

Reflections

What did I learn? What did I gain from all this?

The challenges I faced from music lessons to piano recitals pushed me to develop myself in ways I didn't know were possible. And while I faced these challenges with uncertainty, I chose not to allow fear into my being. Deep in my subconscious mind, deep in my soul, I knew these experiences were happening for a reason. I knew there was a higher power that granted me the ability to play without the need for physical sight. And God knew the reason why. I evolved from being a shy little girl afraid to walk into a room full of people to a self-confident young woman. I thank Mrs. Stevens, my parents, Granny, and my musical experiences for this gift of personal growth.

Losing my vision also taught me to trust myself, and to trust my abilities, not just playing the piano but in other areas of my life. I became aware of my other talents and gifts and that awareness served me well in school.

CHAPTER FOUR

The Fight of My Life (Age 19)

Paralysis Unveils the Power of Prayer

When my parents split up, I was separated from my dad for seven years, the teen years. So many experiences and changes occurred during this time in my life and my dad wasn't there to be a part of them. In many ways, it was an incredibly sad time for me, yet I would learn very quickly to take that energy and redirect it into something else. That something else was my academic studies.

I remember as a little girl before I even started school, Dad would show me how to count with an abacus. He taught me addition, subtraction, and multiplication, all with an abacus. There were no shortages of books in our home on every subject you can imagine. Often, I wonder what would have happened if my dad had had a different path in life; if he wasn't raised by a mother who became a widow when her four sons were all under the age of seven. If his childhood hadn't been so rough, I feel he could have been a schoolteacher because Dad was a walking encyclopedia. He could talk about any subject. When I was around five years old, he would show me blueprints of some of the equipment and engines he was working on. We would walk through a 3D diagram on the paper, section by section. By the time I turned seven, I was reading those blueprints, and cutting out house floor plans from the Saturday Toronto Star newspaper 'Home of the Week' section. If I didn't like the floor plan, I would get a sheet of paper and redraw it. Dad's love for engineering rubbed off on me and by age nine I wanted to be an architect and design and build things. I also had a love for reading, doing jigsaw puzzles, and crossword puzzles, anything that stimulated my mind.

The confidence I gained through music lessons and performing carried over into my school life. Between the ages of nine and 16, I skipped three grades in school. Yes, three. I am not sure why, but life always seemed to move a little slower than I wanted it to, or perhaps I had to move quickly as I always felt my time here was short. In any event, I started causing havoc in the class when I got bored, which was often. I began yawning in class or interrupting teachers by asking "too many" questions. One day in Grade Nine, I almost got sent to the principal's office. I was sitting in math class and the teacher was drawing different triangles on the chalkboard. I yawned, perhaps a little too loud. He walked over to my desk and asked if I had seen this before.

I replied, "Yes, last year." *Why did I open my mouth?* I must have struck a nerve, as I watched his face turn red and he snapped, "No, you could not have seen this, this is Grade Nine math." The challenge began.

I stood up, walked over to the chalkboard, and named each type of triangle: isosceles, right angle, scalene. I went on to explain how to calculate the degrees of each angle, and then I returned to my seat. His face was still red. When the class ended, he told me to remain seated while everyone left.

"Dawn, how do you know this?" he asked.

I explained that I had skipped a grade in elementary school and by Grade Eight, my teacher had given me the Grade Nine textbooks so I wouldn't be bored in class.

He then asked which Grade Nine subjects had I studied in Grade Eight.

"All of them," I replied.

The next day I wrote a four-hour surprise test, unbeknownst to even my parents, and the following month I was transferred to Grade Ten. I was 13.

By the time I turned 16 I had completed high school and started university just shy of turning 17. Imagine, a 16-year-old on a university campus with 19 and 20-year-olds. That was unheard of back in the 80s. Fortunately for me, I was always taller than the average girl and more mature than most, as I had socialized with adults all my life. I didn't mention my age much and no one asked.

My dad missed so many events including my high school music concerts and my awards for accounting and math. He would have been proud to know I studied drafting in school, as I held on to visions of becoming an architect. He missed my first dance and my first date. I started coop work at age 15, which would eventually lead me to a career in accounting. Who knew? There I was, 19 years old, a few weeks away from becoming a university grad, wondering… *Where is my dad? I want him to be part of this milestone in my life.*

I spoke with him a few times a year: on his birthday, my birthday, Christmas, and other special occasions. The last I had heard from him was over a year before and his former telephone number was not in service. I had no way to call him and rumour had it that he was working in western Canada in Alberta or British Columbia.

I missed his smile. I missed his hugs. I sat on my bed that Saturday afternoon wondering if I would see him before graduation. I wanted to see him *now*. I lay very still on my bed and stared intensely out the window at the clouds. *Dad, where are you?* I cleared my mind of anything and everything except the question, *Daddy, where are you? I need to see you. I need to see you now.*

You know that feeling just before you fall asleep when you are drifting in a fog, partially conscious and partially dreaming? I was floating in that vibration when it happened. I felt a gust of wind begin to swirl around me, but I was no longer lying on my bed — I was out of my physical body, outside the window. I looked down to see the outdoor pool, the parking lot, the neighbouring homes, and condominiums. That familiar childhood feeling of playing 'hopscotch' returned to me. I was free to go wherever I wanted. Without hesitation or a second thought, I headed west to find my dad. I was a little rusty, but I focused my intention on getting to the Rocky Mountains to look for my dad. I don't know how long I was away from my physical body and at that moment, I didn't care how long it took. I needed to find him.

Insight - Astral Projection

Now, if you're wondering if it is possible to separate the body from the consciousness, it is if you believe in astral travel. Astral travel is an esoteric term used to describe the ability to intentionally create an out-of-body experience (OBE). It is believed that there are seven planes of existence: physical, astral, mental, spiritual, divine, and logoic planes.

I was gone for quite some time as I travelled to Alberta and then continued west to British Columbia. There was no sign of him anywhere. I was disappointed, sad, and tired. I headed back home to Toronto, Ontario, to my bedroom in our condominium on the seventh floor. I began the descent into my body and was startled to discover I wasn't alone when I returned to my bedroom.

As my body lay on the bed facing the window, I saw a translucent, almost see-through arm wrapped around my waist. *What the hell is going on?!* I snapped back, now fully conscious, into my body, and tried to grab that translucent arm to push it away from me. I couldn't hold it. From the shape of the arm and hand, I could tell it was male, but to this day, I've never seen its face. Both arms were now wrapped a little tighter around my waist, as it pressed up behind me, still facing the window as I lay on my left side. If you have ever seen someone doing the Heimlich Manoeuver, pressing deep into your abdomen, between your navel and your rib cage, that is what it felt like this thing was trying to do to me. The pressure was getting stronger and the more I fought, the more painful it got. The pain spread past my abdomen, around to my lower back. I struggled there on the bed, trying to rock from side to side to shake it the hell off me. *Let go of me. Leave me alone.* The more I struggled with it, the more acute the pain was in my lower back. I couldn't push it off or pull those arms away from my body. I had never felt so much pain in my life! My body was flooded with pain and I couldn't stand it much longer. I desperately wanted to cry but could not. I wanted to yell, hoping my mother, sitting in the living room watching TV, would hear me but I couldn't make a sound. I was petrified as I felt a sword-like object penetrate my tailbone. The pain was excruciating! *God help me. I cannot let this thing get inside me. No way! Please make it stop!* Then, like the first drop of rain falling on my forehead, I suddenly remembered the words to a prayer my mother and I would say:

Psalm 121, KJV

I will lift up mine eyes unto the hills, from whence cometh my help.

² My help cometh from the Lord, which made heaven and earth.

³ He will not suffer thy foot to be moved: he that keepeth thee will not slumber.

⁴ Behold, he that keepeth Israel shall neither slumber nor sleep.

⁵ The Lord is thy keeper: the Lord is thy shade upon thy right hand.

⁶ The sun shall not smite thee by day, nor the moon by night.

⁷ The Lord shall preserve thee from all evil: he shall preserve thy soul.

⁸ The Lord shall preserve thy going out and thy coming in from this time forth, and even for evermore.

By the time I spoke verse 7 in my head, the intruder vanished into thin air.

What the fuck?!

Stunned and speechless, I grabbed my pillow and wept. I wept because I'd been violated and tormented. I wept from my exhaustion from fighting that thing. Little did I know that my fight was not yet over. As I lay on the bed, my pillow soaking wet from crying, my body felt numb. I couldn't feel my legs, my buttocks, or my waist... I was dead numb. *What the hell is going on?* I attempted to sit up when I suddenly realized I wasn't able to move my legs whatsoever. I wanted to scream, but no sound could be made.

Oh God no, not again. I cannot take this. What the hell is wrong with me? First, I lost my hearing, then my speech, my sight, and now this shit?

I was deeply angry, and I turned that anger to God:

You created me and you fucked up, and now I am here suffering.

What the hell did I do to deserve all this?

How much more do you think I can handle?

What do you want from me?

Christ, I cannot move my legs!

In times when I felt my back up against a wall, my natural reaction was to get into 'fight mode' because being afraid and giving up were not options I could live with.

So what did I do?

The only things available to me at that moment were my arms. Despite my anger, I calmed down long enough to use my arms to reach over and twist my upper body as far as I could, enough to get my body to drop to the floor.

I cannot tell you what that felt like hearing my body go 'thump' on the floor, but luckily the only bright light in this sad state I found myself in, was that our floor was covered wall-to-wall, in carpet. I dug my fingers into the carpet and used all the strength in my arms to drag myself towards the bedroom door, like actor Owen Wilson crawling on the ground in the movie *Behind Enemy Lines*.

Do not give up now.

When I finally got to my bedroom door, I made a fist and banged that door as loud as I could, until finally my mom heard me and walked into my room. There she found me lying on the floor, paralyzed from the waist down.

Reflections: Possession and Protection

It would take me another 20 years to fully understand what had taken place in my bedroom that day. They say when the student is ready the teacher appears.

After I woke up spiritually in 2003, many gifted people and Lightworkers began to appear in my life. What seemed like random meetings became divine interventions and connections. One of those connections was a lady named Abigail who had the gift of clairaudience. She could hear and understand the language of angels. Abigail was also a musician and I had attended one of her recitals where she played the harp. As luck would have it, she lived only 3 km from our house. I visited her once for an angel reading, however, what I received was much more than a reading. Abigail knew that I liked to astral travel, and by the time I had met her, I was travelling a lot, almost daily. She was the first person to explain to me the dangers of leaving one's body unattended. She also explained that there were entities on the astral plane – some were of the light and some were dark – and the dark entities would like nothing better than to possess a human body. The biggest advice she gave me was to protect myself before I travelled. I could protect myself by raising my vibration through meditation, wearing crystals, smudging with sage, the sound of crystal bowls, and prayer.

Prayer?

I asked her point-blank, "Is that what happened to me when I was 19? Was a dark entity trying to possess me?

"Yes," she replied.

"And by saying my Psalms I was able to banish it?"

"Yes," she replied.

"Dawn, you need to be grounded. Can I ask you why you astral travel?"

"Because *I can* ever since I was a young child," I replied.

"That is not a reason, my dear. You need to have a purpose. Do not go out without a purpose or you may find yourself in a similar predicament."

No, no, no. I don't think so. I was not about to make that mistake again. I decided at that moment that I would not 'travel' again without a purpose and without raising my vibration before I left.

Insights: Another Fighter

So, what happened that day when my mom walked into my room and saw me laying on the floor face down, unable to walk?

Mom reacted like she always reacted, in a calm manner without question, without any great emotional drama. The morning when she learned I couldn't hear a thing, she wrote a note and sent me off to school. When I played my first recital, blind as a bat, it was Mom who lent me her arm and guided me back to my seat. She was a gentle and loving soul. We got closer with each passing year, especially the years when my dad was gone. My mom eventually became my confidante and best friend. She was there for me for all my pivotal moments throughout my childhood.

Yet on this day, she would need to be more than my mom. She would need to join me in this fight if I were to ever walk again. Mom stood over me for what seemed like several minutes, in silence.

"Mom, what am I going to do? I think we need to go to the hospital."

"Just a minute," were the first words she said to me.

She walked to her bedroom and a few moments later she returned to my room with three things. I recognized two of those things as she placed them on the floor and sat beside me; one was a candle and the other was Tiger Balm. Tiger Balm is a topical medication used to alleviate pain. Its primary ingredients include camphor and menthol. Sometimes when I had a terrible cough, Mom would rub this on my back and chest. At first, it felt extremely hot, and then a cooling sensation would follow in the area where you rubbed it. The third thing she brought with her was a small book with a light blue cover which I had never seen before.

Still lying face down, Mom slid a pillow under my head so I could be more comfortable.

"Do not worry. God is with us," she said.

Mom proceeded to light the candle, open her little blue book, and started reading aloud. They were prayers. Prayers I had never heard before. Her words flowed with ease and her voice felt soothing. Once again, she hushed the storm that was raging in my head with her gentle voice. I don't know how long we were there, but the room became darker as the sun began to set.

Then Mom started to tell me about God's kingdom. She explained that there were some things of the Light and things not of the Light. You either walked with God or walked alone, in the dark.

I tried to follow her story but still found myself confused by what that had to do with my situation.

"Dawn there is nothing to fear when you walk with God," she explained.

Mom leaned over me to roll my shirt up and apply Tiger Balm to my upper and lower back. I didn't feel anything, no heat, no cooling sensation; I simply inhaled that familiar fragrance of camphor and menthol. As she slid down towards my feet, I could only imagine that she was rubbing Tiger Balm down the back of both legs, right down to the soles of my feet.

And then my mom did something strange, she placed the palms of her hands on my upper back between my shoulder blades. I could feel the weight of her hands and the warmth of her touch.

She repeated, "Dawn there is nothing to fear when you walk with God. Just rest now."

I am not sure how long she had her hands on my back, but what I do remember was the *warmth* of her gentle touch. Her hands became warmer and warmer and I melted into it like cold butter on a warm slice of toast. I simply relaxed my body and melted into this welcome, loving, warm feeling. It filled my chest, circled my shoulders and neck, and like a waterfall, this warm energy cascaded down my arms. I began drifting off, almost about to fall asleep...when I felt it. A steady pulsation in my back startled me, as it almost felt like the same pressure I had experienced earlier that afternoon.

"Mom, something is happening!" I shouted.

"I know Dawny, it's OK. Be still."

Then I felt my mom's hands slide down my back right over my tailbone. She stopped. The prayers resumed once more. Her words were steady and firmer now. They didn't sound gentle like they did when she usually prayed. I waited and waited. The candle had melted down to its last inch or two by this time.

I cannot tell you how overwhelmed I was to regain feeling in my back. This was truly a miracle! And by my side, as always, was my mom. I smiled.

"We are not done," she informed me.

Mom moved her hands to my ankles. She placed one hand on each ankle and the prayers resumed.

Have you ever been outside without gloves and your fingers almost freeze, and when you get inside and run warm water on them, they begin to throb and ache? Then you realize it would be better to run cold water on those cold fingers so the blood can rush to them and warm them up? Within seconds of Mom's hands on my ankle, my entire lower body started to ache… a low, pulsating, throbbing pain. The heat moving through my legs stirred up some serious pain.

"It hurts!" I gasped for air. "It really hurts."

"We need to remove it," she said.

"Remove what?" I asked.

"Just a minute…shh."

I wanted to escape the pain, but I had nowhere to hide, nowhere to go. If I could have traded places with anyone at that moment, I would have. The bones in my legs ached, my ankles ached, and my hips ached.

Mom mumbled a few words under her breath and ended with 'so be it'.

That was the first time I heard my mom pray like that, with intensity, conviction, and determination. She was with me in this fight right to the end. And yes, it ended late that night with Mom by my side. She lent me her arms once more, but this time she helped bring me to a standing position. I draped my arms around her like a rag doll, and I held her tight. No words needed to be spoken but she knew how thankful and lucky I felt at that moment to have her in my life. That was the day I discovered my mom was also gifted. How did I not notice this for almost 20 years? She had a healing touch! How many times did she place her hands on my back while I coughed at night, to get me to stop coughing long enough to fall asleep? How many times did she place her hands on the top of my head when it got hot at my piano recitals and I couldn't see?

"Mom, what did you say before you said 'so be it'?"

"Honey, we must pray and keep God close to us."

I recited Psalm 23, a prayer of protection, and a reminder that with God, our enemies will be defeated.

Psalm 23 KJV:

The Lord is my shepherd; I shall not want.

[2] He maketh me to lie down in green pastures: he leadeth me beside the still waters.

[3] He restoreth my soul: he leadeth me in the paths of righteousness for his name's sake.

[4] Yea, though I walk through the valley of the shadow of death, I will fear no evil: for thou art with me; thy rod and thy staff they comfort me.

[5] Thou preparest a table before me in the presence of mine enemies: thou anointest my head with oil; my cup runneth over.

[6] Surely goodness and mercy shall follow me all the days of my life: and I will dwell in the house of the Lord forever.

On this day, I was introduced to the power of prayer and a new perspective of what it meant to walk with God and have no fear. Mom believed in this higher power we call God and her strong belief turned into the faith that I would be healed. My mom was a healer and a fighter in her own right, and she stood by me through all my trials and tribulations. She was my anchor, a spiritual warrior!

CHAPTER FIVE

Fuck No

Celibacy Unveils True Love

How do you ease into a topic about sex? You don't. Sex can be raw, passionate, and even animalistic. Bodies creating friction, sweating, sounds, moaning, you get the picture. Ha! I didn't get the picture or the memo for quite some time. I was a late bloomer on many levels when it came to boys, dating, and sex. My naivety and lack of interest drove several male suitors into a frenzy, some left agitated, and a few left heartbroken. However, there would be three men of significance in my life from my teen years into my early twenties that would shape and influence my transition from a girl to a woman.

Growing up, most of my friends were male. I had one or two close female friends but not too many. I had a competitive nature and loved competing with the boys, especially in academics. I was the only girl who studied drafting at my high school, and I was one of two girls that took shop instead of home economics. Scandalous, right? I always loved to design and build things, ever since my dad and I would study blueprints and house floor plans together. My heart was set on being an architect from a young age. I started high school on the verge of my 13th birthday, and later, while most of my classmates from Grade Nine were finishing high school, I got my diploma and started university at 16. Perhaps, I was an early bloomer from the shoulders up? My body finally caught up to my classmates during my last year of high school as I blossomed from a flat-chested, long-legged, skinny girl to a 5-foot, 8-inch hour-glass shaped girl with a 34" bust – 23" waist – 34" hips. I vaguely remember starting to pay attention to boys more when I started high school, especially when we had to go to dances, and during slow dancing.

Growing up I thought guys were silly and, well, dumb. They seemed so obsessed with getting physical and that was a big turn-off for me. How can you want to get physical with someone you barely know? And the lines, oh those lines! I swear the boys in high school read the same secret handbook on what to say until they got a yes from a girl!

Here are some of the lines I heard while slow dancing:

"Baby, I think you are the one."

The one for what? The one for this week? Negro, please.

"You know, I have been watching you for a long time and I think it's time to get to know you better."

I would cool that off with, "Sorry, I don't date *men*." (LOL)

"You are so fine. I think we could make some beautiful babies."

Hell No...STD walking, time to go.

And a replay from another guy:

"You are so fine. I think we could make some beautiful babies."

My reply, "No glove, no love, sugar."

And his comeback:

"I have the glove and you need my love, sugar."

Shit! Step back, Dawn. Leave some Christian distance, this one ain't playing.

What is Christian distance you might ask? About four inches between his waist and mine.

During my senior year of high school, I met Jay. Someone had posted on the school bulletin board that they needed a math tutor. Math was my favourite subject, and I had a light course load the first semester, so I thought, why not. I love teaching others to learn new things. I called the number and Jay and I arranged to meet right after school. I asked him which math he needed help with, algebra or calculus.

"All of it," he said, looking bewildered.

"Ok, let's start with algebra as it is the easier of the two."

We agreed on a schedule during school hours, where he would meet me when I was in study hall when his schedule gelled with mine. Over the next few weeks, we worked together. I learned a few things about him and discovered we had some things in common. We both liked music. He introduced me to reggae music and I introduced him to classical. We both enjoyed reading, watching basketball, and walking. After math tutoring, we started walking home together after school, and to my surprise, he lived one block away from me. I could almost see his apartment building from my balcony. Our friendship grew.

Until that point, I had never taken the time to make close friends. I had moved so much while I was a child, I stopped wanting to have a best friend because in no time Dad would want to move again. Now, some may say I had a lonely childhood. I was an only child who attended four elementary schools and two high schools and was a loner by choice. But as I said before, playing the piano was my soother. It brought me joy. Music was a safe place I could lose myself in for hours at a time and for many years, music became and was my best friend. It filled many voids and gave me everything I needed. *Well, almost everything.*

After a few short months, Jay and I became best friends. There was an innocence about him, and I liked that. Despite being teenagers, I always felt like we were young children, just enjoying each other's company. We would often eat at each other's homes. Both of our moms were amazing cooks, so we were well fed. We went to the movies, took many long walks at parks, and we would talk for hours at a time about so many things. He even let me cut his hair once (oops, big mistake). Both our dads were absent and our mothers were overprotective. Jay was a great listener and had a dry sense of humour, which made me laugh a lot. We talked seven days a week. I was very fond of him and loved the companionship. Two loners and only children who drifted towards each other and now we were each other's best friend.

I remember one spring day, he walked me home after school, and as I turned to him to say see you tomorrow, he leaned into my face and planted a kiss on my cheek!

Startled I asked, "Why did you do that?"

"Because (big smile)."

I tossed and turned that night. Something was stirring inside that I didn't like. The next evening I called him, and we talked for almost two hours about that kiss on the cheek, and what that might turn into. I didn't want our friendship to change, or so I thought. After a long debate on the phone, we both agreed that our friendship was too important to ruin it with a kiss or dating.

The high school year came to an end, at least for me, as he had two more years to go. I started university and continued to hang out with Jay, not every day, but regularly. Many nights when I had a computer lab that ended quite late, there he was waiting outside the main doors to walk me home. We were truly best friends. I was there for him and he was there for me. By year two of university, our feelings grew too strong to ignore as our bond of friendship evolved into something more and we talked about going on a date. I was almost 18. For our first date, we chose to have a picnic lunch at a national park. We walked hand in hand until we found the perfect spot to have our picnic. We ate and laughed and did some people watching. Then it got quiet. As we sat on the blanket, Jay moved closer and put his arm around my waist. And we had our first official date kiss. Awkward? A little, at first, but nice. As we kissed, we decided to get more comfortable and laid down on the blanket. I rolled from my side onto my back and he repositioned himself to lay on top of me as the kissing continued.

"Ouch," I squeaked.

"What is it?" he asked.

"I got poked."

"What? I would not… I didn't…"

"No, silly," I replied. "I think there's a plastic fork under the blanket and it poked me in the back."

We both burst out laughing which interrupted the romance and sat up and thought how silly we both must look.

When the laughter faded, Jay got more serious and asked, "Well, where do we go from here?"

I sat there pondering what to say. *Should I speak from my heart or my head? Maybe it would have been easier if we had started out dating instead of becoming best friends.*

"Jay, I think we have more to lose if we get romantic and it doesn't work out. There's no turning back if we change what we have. We are each other's best friends and I think it's safer to keep it that way."

"What are you really afraid of? You know I love you."

After an exceptionally long (pregnant) pause, I replied, "I love you too, but I don't want either of us to get hurt."

What do we gain, what do we lose? Love is complicated, no doubt. In our hearts, we loved each other and would do anything for each other, but for me, romantic love was simply not in the cards.

We continued to hang out, although a little less frequently. It was noticeably more difficult to ignore the physical and sexual tension that was brewing between us. At the start of my last year of university, I took the easy way out and wrote him a letter about how I felt and why I thought it would be best to stop seeing each other. The letter ended with, "I do not want either of us to end up being hurt." I sealed that envelope with my tears. I slowly walked across the street as if I were in a funeral procession, up to his apartment floor, and slid the tear-stained envelope under the door. The next day he did the same. I found an envelope under my front door, but what he wrote was much shorter than mine. "Too late. I am already hurt by your letter. Love always, Jay." I laid on my bed and cried for hours.

Have you ever ended a close relationship and it felt like a part of your body was missing, like you had a limb amputated? For weeks I felt like I was walking in a daze, completely out of balance. This was my first heartbreak. The grief I felt from walking away from my best friend impacted me physically, causing my thyroid to go into overdrive. Little did I know at the time, that it would become a physical pattern in my life whenever I experienced deep sadness or grief.

Despite feeling sad, I worked hard at convincing myself I had done the right thing. We were two late bloomers with no experience (both virgins) trying to sort out feelings of emotional love, physical love, and the love of a best friend. Remember the movie *Blue Lagoon*, where two innocent children got shipwrecked, and as they approached their teen years, they started to explore each other? Yup, the blind leading the blind and the girl gets pregnant. No, thank you! What was I afraid of? Giving him all of me, my heart, body, and soul, and crossing the point of no return!

So, what did I do?

I found a diversion.

In my last year of university, I began to socialize *a lot*, attending university events, going to dance clubs, movies, dinners, and concerts, with both male and female friends. I also decided in my last year, at the age of 19, to close the chapter on playing the piano with the Royal Conservatory of Music. I had more activities competing for my attention. It was also during my last year at university that I decided to get a job so I could reduce my student debt before I graduated. My part-time job took up 25 hours a week. Essentially, I worked Tuesday, Thursday, and Saturday, and I went to school on Monday, Wednesday, and Friday. This schedule didn't leave me much time to socialize. Still, I crammed in as much as I could on the weekends, and in time, Jay became a memory.

The son of a family friend, named Michael, worked at the same company I did. As my shift ended, Michael's shift would begin. We often passed each other between the bus stop and the building like two ships in the night. One evening as I was leaving, our eyes met. Michael smiled at me and asked, "Can I walk you to the bus stop?"

With a serious look on my face, I snapped and said, "No need, the stop is right over there. I got legs; they work."

He smiled, more of a grin I think, and said, "OK, Miss Dawn, maybe tomorrow."

And that is how it began…every Tuesday and Thursday, Michael would offer to walk me to the bus stop and my reply would be the same, "No, thanks."

This went on for several weeks but guys can be persistent.

One evening, Michael couldn't help it and stopped in my path so that I had to stop walking. "I see you walking so fast, always in a hurry. Even when you finish work you walk like you are on a mission. What do you do for fun?"

Sigh... "I dance," I replied.

His big grin reappeared. "Would you like to go out dancing with me one night? It's not like I'm a stranger...our families know each other."

As the bus approached my stop, I started running (*Dawn, that is rude*). I quickly turned to answer, "I only go out on Saturdays," and without even thinking, I smiled back. *Oops.* On my next workday, we exchanged phone numbers. Well, after that first dance, Michael began calling me every day. On the days I was in school, he made every effort to drive me to my first class or pick me up after my last class. He was suave, smooth, charismatic, and was always a gentleman. Before I knew it, we were going out exclusively, to concerts and movies and the like. So, it was very natural and logical that Michael would be my date for university graduation.

However, a second man would also join me at graduation – my dad. Yes, Dad had called Mom a few weeks after my astral projection incident. He called to ask my mom's permission to attend my graduation. It was Dad who'd filed for divorce, not Mom, and they didn't talk very often. Now he wanted to be there for this major milestone, not only in my life but our family, as I was the first one of his brother's children to graduate from university and that was a big deal. Can you imagine...my dad brought four cameras and his tripod to my graduation ceremony. It was a perfect day!

I was so excited to see him again and for him to meet Michael, who was slowly but surely becoming part of our family. After the graduation ceremony, the four of us went out to dinner. Michael was quite a conversationalist and very personable. He was a people person and an extrovert, and I could understand why he chose a career in sales.

I didn't make it easy on Michael when we first started dating. About two months into dating we went to a concert and after the concert, we walked back to his car. Typically, Michael would open my door like a gentleman and then walk around and get in the driver's seat. But after this concert, he walked to the passenger side and stood there like a statue, just watching me with a puzzled look on his face.

"What's the matter?" I asked. "Why do you look so serious?"

He blurted out, "Don't you have any feelings? We've been going out for two months and we haven't kissed!"

Oh my god, he's keeping track, I thought. Don't get me wrong, I liked him, and we had fun going out, but kissing and hugging and all that steamy stuff never rocked my boat. I also knew Michael had a reputation for being a ladies' man and dated a lot, so I kept my distance. Yet, there he stood in front of me, like a lost puppy in the rain. He walked up to me and wrapped his humongous arms around me. I am a sucker for hugs, especially bear hugs. He smiled and asked, "Can I kiss you?"

I smiled back and replied, "Yes."

Now, I didn't mean for this to happen the way it did. But when Michael kissed me, I immediately thought of Jay (who I hadn't seen for almost nine months) and how *he* kissed me. My feelings were different. *Dawn be present.* I quickly dismissed the comparison and got out of my head...

"That wasn't so bad, right?" Michael asked as he grinned from ear to ear.

"Hmm," I replied, trying to play it cool.

After that first kiss, Michael made every effort to see me every day, even after I started working full-time. I was fortunate to start working a week after graduation and my first job was at the university I had graduated from. Come rain, sleet, snow, or sunshine, Michael was there every day, either to have lunch or pick me up after work to bring me home. He was a gentleman, through and through. Sometimes I had a strange feeling he needed to see me every day to make sure I didn't have time for anyone else, not even my girlfriends. He never pressured me into having sex, but his big one-liner was, "Ain't nothing like the real thing," and we both knew what he meant. My classic reply was, "You cannot want something you never had," and he knew what I meant.

The third most significant man in my life during these years was Carl. Carl knew me from way back before I had met Jay or Michael. We grew up together in a big blended family of my cousins, aunts, uncles, and friends, who worked and socialized together for many years. Carl worked at my cousin's construction business where I was the bookkeeper and every payday, I saw him and the gang to hand them their checks. We regularly attended the same social events, weddings, and the like. I affectionately called Carl my bodyguard, as he often went to the same dance clubs I was at, and used his Spidey senses and eagle eyes to watch me from a distance to keep 'the wolves' at bay. If he ever saw a guy coming on too strong with me on the dance floor (no Christian distancing), he would rush on over to break things up and say, "Excuse me, the lady promised me this dance."

Speaking of 'lady', at every wedding, and I do mean every wedding we attended, whenever they played that song by Lionel Ritchie, we would find ourselves hand-in-hand, dancing together. The song started like this:

"Lady, I'm your knight in shining armour and I love you…"

Now, Carl and I had an understanding that we would always be platonic friends. Besides, I never dated guys shorter than me ever, and he was 5'5" to my 5'8".

Carl watched and observed me from a distance…my crushes, my first heartbreak with Jay, and now, going out with Michael.

I remember a conversation we had about love. I was about to turn 20 and we were dancing at a wedding to our song, "Lady."

"You and Michael seem serious. Do you love him?"

"Do I love him? There are many types of love. I don't know. I like his company."

"Dawn, from where I'm sitting, Michael is serious about you. You know, I hope you don't mind me saying this, but whenever you get close, really start feeling close to someone, you pull away. You have done it all your life. What are you afraid of?"

There was that pregnant pause again.

"I don't want to get hurt," I replied.

"It's like you have a wall around your heart and that's not healthy. I'm worried about you. I want to see you happy and truly in love."

I heard the sincerity in his voice. Carl was a good friend, confidante, and bodyguard.

"Thanks."

The song ended and we returned to our respective social circles.

Carl had attended every birthday party I had since I was 13. When I turned 18, the word on the street was *Dawn is legal, a.k.a. who is going to hit that first?* And a few wolves came out of the woodwork that year. Some guys found sport in trying to deflower a virgin. I recall getting picked up to go to dinner and a movie, and my date showed up in a limo. Yes, a limo. What was he thinking? After the movies, we went to dinner and I noticed he had a drink before we ate and two drinks after. I got a little concerned. Dinner ended and we got in the limo to head home. The limo made a detour and the driver parked the car. As my date moved in closer to me, I could smell the rum on his breath.

"You know, Dawn, I have been watching you for a long time and I think it's time to get to know you better."

Oh God, not this line again.

"Dawn I think I love…" I placed my hand over his mouth.

"No, you don't. That's the rum talking. You're drunk. Please take me home."

He moved in closer and started groping me.

"Stop it, you are drunk," I repeated.

He continued moving his hands all over my body.

"I said, stop!"

Then the truth came out of his lips as his hands finally took a break. "What are you saving it for, marriage? Come on now. I *know* you want me."

I clenched my jaw tight and used all my energy to make a fist and then cuffed him as hard as I could in the centre of his chest. He fell back.

"Take me home right now or I will tell the family what you tried to do tonight."

My cheeks felt hot, my heart pounded …I must have looked like a lion ready to tear his head off. He took one look in my eyes and shifted to the other side of the back seat. He told the driver to take me home.

For the next 25 minutes, we sat in silence until the limo pulled up to my apartment. I turned my head to face him and he looked me in the eyes and said, "I am sorry."

I never saw or spoke to him again. When Carl discovered this guy was a co-worker, he almost got into a fistfight with him at the construction site. Carl continued to be my knight in shining armour until the day I got married.

So, there I was at age 20, celibate, a virgin, dating a guy who was planning to propose. He had met my parents at graduation and I had met his. His dad had a deep Jamaican accent and whenever we visited him he would always say to Michael, "Son, ah queen ya dee get eh? Ya make me proud."

We went from dancing to dating to meeting the parents, and now we had come to this. It was the next logical step, right? Michael proposed one night at dinner. I ordered cheesecake (my favourite dessert at the time) and he told the waiter to bring one slice and two plates and forks. When the plates arrived, the waiter placed the cheesecake in front of Michael, and placed the second plate in front of me, with a little black box on it – just big enough for a ring.

He was visibly nervous as his hands trembled. He reached over and held my hands.

"I can't believe I am saying this. Dawn, would you marry me?"

After a brief pause, I replied, "Yes."

The walls of Jericho began to crumble.

I made a conscious choice to give myself physically to Michael, my fiancé. It would be a fairy tale ending to say I made that choice from a place of love, and we lived happily ever after, but remember I don't believe in fairy tales. I made that choice not from a place of love, but a place of curiosity because I wanted to know what all the fuss was about sex. He was very patient, understanding, and a gentleman.

Reflections: My Heart

They say you never forget your first time. I guess some part of that may be true. I remembered the action, but for the life of me, I do not remember the *feeling*. I do remember feeling free… free of the burden of naivety and wondering. It was done, I was no longer a virgin. I was a woman now.

Soon after, our parents and friends started asking us when the big day would be. The big day? That is the next logical step, right? I began feeling as if I was riding a conveyor belt. You put this thing on, then move here and put this on this. After engagement comes marriage and then… my life was moving on autopilot and that felt foreign to me. Decisions seemed to be out of my hands yet wasn't it me who said yes to the engagement ring? Michael was ecstatic, however, I didn't feel the same. I already knew in my heart that this would not end well. Carl's voice was echoing in my head… 'Whenever you get close to someone you pull away.' *Is that what I am doing again? Am I pulling away as I pulled away from Jay?*

I loved his company and we had fun times, but was that enough for a long-term relationship? Did I want that now? Could I see myself spending the rest of my life with Michael? Something was missing.

I had recently bought a condo for my mom and me, and Michael came over one night to help move several boxes into the storage locker. After an hour or so, we took a well-deserved break and decided to sit on the couch. A few moments later, my phone rang.

"Hello," I said.

"Hi, Dawn."

My heart jumped. Oh my God, it was Jay! I hadn't spoken to him in almost a year and a half.

"I heard the news. Is it true you got engaged?"

"Yes," I replied.

"Can you talk?"

"Not really," I started to feel my face flush.

"I just need to ask you one thing. Do you love him more than you loved me?"

Jesus my eyes were about to reveal a secret that was lodged deep in my heart. So deep that I didn't know it was there until I heard Jay's voice on the phone. Here I was sitting beside my lover, my fiancé, talking to my first love.

I stood up and turned my back to Michael.

"I have to go," I whispered.

I beelined as fast as I could to the bathroom to splash cold water on my face to hold back the tears. *Damn it…too late.* I left the water taps on for a few minutes so Michael wouldn't hear me sob. I grabbed a towel to wipe my face and suddenly stopped. I watched the water drops and teardrops, intertwined, rolling down my cheeks. I watched as the white in my eyes became red from crying. I took a good look in the mirror – an exceptionally long look into my eyes and beyond… into my heart and beyond …. into my soul.

Dawn be honest with yourself. For once, be honest about your feelings.

I looked. I saw. I knew.

I had allowed Michael to have me physically, but he didn't have my heart or soul. I knew who had my heart and I was in denial. I returned to the couch to sit with Michael. He could already see the red veins in my eyes from crying.

"Who was that on the phone?"

A pregnant pause. I said nothing.

"Dawn, please tell me it wasn't that guy from high school."

I looked down and stared at the diamond ring on my finger. *Dawn, what are you doing? Be honest about your feelings.* I slipped the ring off my finger and handed it to Michael. "I am truly sorry, but I can't marry you."

Dead silence oozed into every inch and crevice of that condo. It seeped into the walls and along the floor until the only sound we could hear was each other's heartbeat. Michael was stunned. I got up and walked over to the front door. Michael sat on that couch for what seemed like an eternity. When he finally stood to walk his legs were unsteady. He walked past me, without making eye contact, opened the door, and walked away.

I locked the door and promptly called Jay back.

"Jay, I never meant to hurt you. I hope you can forgive me. You will always be in my heart."

I never saw either of them again until I was married with children.

All Work and No Play

What was I to do now?

The thing I did best.

I poured myself into my work. In addition to my full–time job, I started a part-time job. Mission accomplished, as it kept me physically and mentally busy and emotionally distant from everyone. My dream of becoming an architect faded when I started a bookkeeping practice as my side hustle. Math and accounting always came easy to me in school, so I decided to stick with it. Little did I know it would serve me well for almost two decades.

I worked at my day job from 8 a.m. to 4 p.m., then commuted downtown and did bookkeeping from 6 p.m. to 11 p.m. I went home, fell asleep exhausted, then got up and did it all over again, five days a week for nearly two years. Like my mom, I loved to save my money. A year into my new life, I had saved enough and made enough on the appreciation of the condo, to sell it and buy two homes. My mom was not the risk-taker that I was, but I convinced her we would do better financially to have an investment property, and she went along and co-signed the mortgage papers. Both homes were on the same street. Mom and I lived in one house and I rented the other one. That was my new life: work, sleep and work.

Carl would call me now and again to catch up. He knew to only call on Saturday or Sunday when I was home and not working. We agreed to meet for brunch one Sunday. He knew I loved pancakes so we met at a place that made lumberjack pancakes. They called it that because each pancake was about 12 inches in diameter. Mmm mmm, good.

Carl arrived before me and when he saw me walk in, his jaw dropped.

"Girl, what is going on, where is the rest of you?" He twirled me around like we were dancing.

I had lost about 20 pounds over the two years, eating on the run, often skipping dinners to get to my second job, then coming home too late with little appetite.

"Nothing wrong with being slim and trim," I answered.

"Are you trying to fatten me up with pancakes?" I asked.

"Well you know, there is more bounce to the ounce. Girl, eat up!"

We had a nice visit and got caught up. He had met a girl and he thought she was the one. His face lit up every time he mentioned her name. Yup, I could see him married with a couple of kids in no time. Yet once again Carl stated, "Dawn, I am worried about you. You are working way too much. It's not healthy."

"I am good," I insisted.

"What about love?" he inquired. "Aren't you lonely?"

"Ha," I laughed, "I don't have time to be lonely, besides, I've got two mortgage payments and I plan to get a third property next year and..."

He cut me off, shaking his head, "Dawn, Dawn, Dawn. Don't you know all work and no play is just not natural?"

"Who says I don't play? My two girlfriends and I go dancing on the weekends. But you wouldn't know that since we don't see you anymore now that you have *her*." We both chuckled. "I guess you found your 'lady' after all."

"Dawn, I hope you find love one day," he continued.

"Love? Love is overrated, love is for fools who want to have their hearts broken. I don't plan to get married because I don't plan on being divorced. Single life with no kids is what I see in my future. Carl, stop worrying, I am good."

I am not getting married and I am not having kids.

That was my modus operandi until I met *him*.

The Matchmaker Enters

Some people have a knack for numbers while others have the gift of gab. My girlfriend Kaye has a magic gift for pairing people up. She started matchmaking in high school and the three couples she matched from Grade Nine are still going strong today! Kaye and I became friends in Grade Six and she is the only person from childhood that I maintain a friendship with. We were both raised with strong family values in Caribbean households. We shared a lot of our journey, from entering puberty to dating, working, and entering a new era as adults.

One Saturday night, Kaye and my other girlfriend Mary came over to my place. The plan was to chillax, watch a chick flick, and eat popcorn. About half an hour into the movie, Kaye announced, "We should go out. A new club just opened by the Toronto airport, let's go check it out. I hear it's nice."

"Nah, I don't feel like going out. I just want to chill."

"Kaye? Kaye!"

Too late, she went to my closet and picked out an outfit. "I think this would look great." She picked out a skin-tight, white, straight leg jumpsuit, and my candy-striped jacket with the matching shoes. Did I mention I had a shoe fetish? At least 25 pairs, in every colour of the rainbow.

"Don't worry Dawn," Mary added, "that jacket is long enough to cover your assets nicely."

We all started laughing.

I was outnumbered. By the time I got dressed and put on some makeup, my mood had lightened and I was looking forward to dancing.

We drove to the new club. The DJ was on fire playing all the top R&B tunes:

- My Prerogative (Bobby Brown)
- If It Isn't Love (New Edition)
- So Emotional (Whitney Houston)
- I Want to Dance with Somebody (Whitney Houston)
- When Doves Cry (Prince)

He sprinkled them with some soca, reggae, funk, and soul.

The three of us typically danced the fast songs together and then took a breather when the slow songs came on. However, we had an unspoken code that if one of us slow danced with a guy for two songs that was code for, "I need some space to socialize."

The DJ turned up the heat with a soca song and we were jamming on the dance floor when he walked up.

"Do you mind if I join you ladies?" he said softly, looking my way.

Wow, he is a brave one approaching three women at once!

He looked harmless, so we said sure. Now there were four of us grooving to the beats. After two songs, the beat slowed down with some reggae tunes. Mary and I went to sit and get a drink, while Kaye stayed on the dance floor with him.

Two reggae songs later they were still dancing so we gave her some space. It looked like they were talking. When the fast songs resumed, Kaye and our brave soul went to sit in a quiet area to continue their conversation. Mary and I returned to dancing. We must have danced for about half an hour, non-stop, but by then those four-inch heels I was wearing needed a break. He and Kaye were still talking but it was getting late, so we walked up to them.

"Time to break this up, you two, we got to head home."

"Break what up?" asked Kaye.

Kaye grabbed my arm as she said excuse me to our mystery man, "We need to go to the ladies' room."

"We do? Ok."

As soon as we got in the ladies' room she started to explain, "Dawn, he has been asking me about you this whole time."

"Me? Why? What is he asking?"

"How long have I known you, what do you do, a bunch of things. Why didn't you come over to save me?"

"Save you! I thought you two had something bubbling." I replied.

Well, that took me by surprise. I thought he liked Kaye.

We returned and Kaye formally introduced us, "Dawn this is Ian. Ian, Dawn."

"Ian James," he said as he reached over and shook my hand.

It was the first time I really looked at him after he approached us on the dance floor. He had a pleasant face, I felt a gentle spirit and those eyes...those brown eyes locked with mine and seemed eerily familiar, and all I could see in those beautiful brown eyes was a sea of kindness.

"Ladies and gentlemen, it's closing time!" the bartender announced.

The four of us headed out, Mary and Kaye intentionally walking faster to give Ian and me some space.

"Can I walk you to your car?"

"Sure."

"Do you have a boyfriend?"

OMG, 20 questions.

"Perhaps," I replied.

"Does that mean I can call you or…?"

"How can you call me? You don't know my number."

He smiled.

"Sorry. My number is unlisted. Nice meeting you." I quickly replied and scooted into my car.

Yup, hard to get because I had a modus operandi to uphold, remember? No marriage, no kids, single for life.

The three of us drove off.

"Well? Did you give him your number?" Kaye inquired.

"No. Why would I do that?" I asked.

However, for the next few days, I couldn't get his face out of my mind. Like a boomerang, it kept showing up, those brown eyes, his nose, his lips, every curve of his face like he was standing in front of me. By now, my mom sensed I was a little restless.

"What's the matter, Dawny?"

"I can't get his face out of my mind."

The phone suddenly rang. It was Kaye, with great excitement in her voice, "Dawn, I got his number, do you want it?"

"How did you get Ian's number?"

"From a mutual friend. Do you have a pen? Write it down."

"Kaye, I am not calling him!"

"416…" she continued, ignoring what I had just said.

I wrote it down.

I sat there for another hour looking at the numbers I had written. I was not calling him. Call me old-fashioned but girls simply do not call guys.

Mom walked by, again sensing I was flustered.

"Dawn, are you calling him as a friend or something else? If it's as a friend what is the harm in calling? You got to know, child." And she walked away.

Five more days went by, and for five days Kaye called to find out if I had called him yet. Miss Matchmaker was stirring her magic pot.

On day six, I called him. A girl answered.

"Hi, my name is Dawn, and I am calling for Ian."

She covered the phone but not too well, as I heard her shout, "Mom, a girl is calling for Ian!"

"Child, tell your brother he has a phone call," another female voice replied.

"Hi," he said, "sorry about the wait."

"No worries. How are you?" I asked.

"Good, nice to hear your voice again."

Ahem. Looking for brownie points already.

"Kaye gave me your number. I guess you two have mutual friends."

He went on to explain the connection, and quickly added, "I would have called you sooner if I had your number."

Without hesitation, I asked, "Do you have a pen? My number is 416…but I don't take calls during weekdays, only on the weekends."

"Ok, noted."

"What are you doing next weekend?" The words popped out of my mouth without any filter. *Dawn, what are you doing? Modus operandi, remember?*

"Next weekend I am out of town, at a competition."

"Competition, what do you do?"

"I am on the Canadian Track and Field team and we have trials next weekend, but the weekend after would be great to meet if you are free."

"Yes, that will work. What did you have in mind?"

"Let me surprise you."

I quietly smiled to myself. Mystery man wants to surprise me. "Ok, talk then."

First dates are always memorable. This one was not only memorable, but it was also comical. All he told me was that we were going out to dinner. I got dolled up in a peach coloured dress, wearing three-inch heels with a matching clutch purse. Yes, I loved my high heel shoes.

The doorbell rang. Mom answered as I walked towards the door.

My first words… "What? You are wearing shorts!" I blurted out.

There he stood, wearing a navy-blue shirt, beige walking shorts, and sandals. *Lord, sandals for a dinner date.*

He could see I wasn't pleased.

"Sorry…Ian this is my mom, Mom, this is Ian James."

I quickly adjusted my attitude so as not to ruin the date and hoped I wasn't too late. "Hold on," I said, and I ran to my room, slipped off my heels, and put on a pair of sandals.

"Ok, let's go."

Despite the wardrobe drama, we had a fabulous evening. He took me to a delightful seafood place with the most delicious menu. As I sat across from him at dinner, watching every curve of his face with my eyes locked on those beautiful brown eyes, I thought, have I seen those eyes before?

After dinner, we walked by the lake downtown for what seemed like hours. Walking and talking. Funny, I made all that fuss about his shoes earlier, and now I was relieved I had switched to sandals. We strolled hand in hand, and the energy I felt from him was gentle and made me feel safe. By the time he dropped me home, a little part of me, somewhere deep inside, implicitly trusted him. Imagine, trusting a total stranger! I could not explain it.

As soon as I got home the phone rang.

"Well, how was it?"

"Kaye, do you know what time it is?"

"Yeah, but when I called earlier your mom told me you two had gone out. Well, how was it?"

"It was nice. Nicer than nice."

"Mm hum, Ok," she replied.

Things moved like we were gliding on ice. By the fourth date, we were talking about how many kids were an ideal number to have. We agreed that three was the right number. What happened to my modus operandi, single for life?

On our fifth date, he surprised me with a gorgeous blue star sapphire ring. "A friendship ring," he explained.

When I told Kaye about the ring, she said, "Mm hum, Ok."

By date six, the friendship ended. We returned from the movies and were sitting in the car talking when he said, "I know you like to keep to yourself. You are a smart, independent, beautiful woman. But I want you to know I will never hurt you. One day, we'll be sitting together on a porch remembering this conversation tonight when I told you, we are going to grow old together. You are the only woman for me, and I thank God I found you."

Those five words echoed in my head and my heart as I looked into those beautiful brown eyes…I will never hurt you.

"Can I kiss you?" he asked.

I nodded yes.

And what a perfect kiss it was. The friendship ended that night. He stole my heart and my soul with that one kiss. I trusted him and I knew without any doubt that he would never hurt me. A month later we got engaged. Everything just felt right, and we fit together like hand in glove, body, heart, and soul.

He proposed the day before he was to fly to Seoul to compete in the 1988 Olympics. That year was the first time I watched the opening ceremonies, every track and field event, and the closing ceremonies. I was so proud of him and what he had accomplished. He would go on to qualify for two more Olympics: Barcelona in 1992 and Atlanta in 1996. To this day, I tease him that marriage improved his long jump.

Now, back to 1988. By the time he returned from Seoul we both knew the wedding date was going to change. We planned a family road trip with his parents and my mom. His parents had been married almost 30 years and were the sweetest couple I had ever met. On the first night of our road trip, we told them we were moving the wedding date up from June 1989 to November 1988. Both moms looked stunned, and his mom asked me, point-blank, "Are you pregnant?"

"Mom, no," Ian intervened. "It's nothing like that. We love each other and we want to make it official now. Why wait?"

His dad sat quietly, head down, smiling. He knew his son was in love and he was happy for us. Like an old married man, his dad waited quietly for the moms to sort it all out. Our parents knew us to be level-headed sensible people, and they gave us their blessings. So, there you have it, from our first date to our wedding date, four months had passed. Yes, four.

My matchmaker friend, Kaye maintained her 100% batting average. This year, 2021, marks 33 amazing years of marriage. And to that, her humble reply to this day remains, "Mm hum, Ok."

Reflection - Soul Mates

Once I began writing books, I became a public speaker and started teaching workshops all over the country. I hosted a one-day workshop in Newmarket, Ontario, on a beautiful farm property with a labyrinth and had driven there the night before to get settled and set up early on Saturday before our attendees arrived. I had heard from other energy practitioners that the owner of the farm was a gifted intuitive. After dinner, we sat in her living room in front of a ginormous stone fireplace enjoying tea and chit chat. I soon discovered what her gift was. We were talking about our children as mothers often do when I mentioned my eldest daughter's name.

"She chose him again to be her father," she explained, as she stared into space.

"Excuse me?"

"Your daughter. It's the second time your husband has been her father... They have a soul contract. She died young last time; a young bride. He felt guilty that he could not protect her last time. This time he will protect her, she will live much longer."

"A soul contract? And she picked him?"

Fuck No

"Yes. What is your husband's name?"

"It's Ian. Ian James."

"One…two… three… four… five… you two keep finding each other. Six…"

"Why are you counting?"

"You two keep finding each other. At least six times you have been a couple."

"What? Six times! Are you serious?"

She went on to describe the countries and the timelines we had been together in, reuniting every so often. She was more than clairvoyant; I think she was a time traveller as well. What the hell? Now I was staring into space. Could that be true? Did Ian and I have a soul contract to reunite again and again?

His eyes, those familiar brown eyes…feeling safe… instant trust I never felt with anyone before. We fit just right, no drama. We flowed together in life with ease, we wanted the same things, we valued the same things. We met and married in four months. Who does that? Perhaps it was true, we are soul mates. That would explain a lot.

"Ha," I chuckled, remembering what Ian told me on date six, the night he kissed me: *You are the only woman for me, and I thank God I found you.*

No, thank God we found each other, again.

Reflections: Sacred Love

I am blessed to have experienced many forms of love in this lifetime. The love of my parents, grandmother, friends, best friend, first love, soul mate, and later, the love of my children and grandchildren.

There are many aspects of love to be enjoyed. I find it a shame that we are socialized to focus on sex more than love. The media seems obsessed about turning people into sex-obsessed objects, influencing what we wear, how we smell, how we socialize. If you are not sex-obsessed, society makes you feel like something is wrong with you. But sex does not equal love. I can live without sex, I did that for 21 years, but can I live without love?

For me, love must be sacred. Even as a teenager, I wasn't interested in casual dating and cheap thrills.

Fuck? No.

I wanted something more, something special, and something sacred.

I wanted a love that transcends the physical and to be with someone who wanted the same, and I am eternally blessed I found him.

CHAPTER SIX

The Tree by the River

Loss of Appetite Unveils New Source of Energy

Psalm 1:3 (NKJV)… like a tree planted by the rivers of water, that brings forth its fruit in its season, whose leaf also shall not wither…

My life became calm after we got married, sprinkled with feelings of intense joy and elation with each new birth. I loved being a mother and observing the wonder and intelligence of those little people. Baby number one arrived 11 months after we got married, then baby number two 16 months later, followed by baby number three 21 months after that. I had all three babies in my twenties. We had our hands full with three children under the age of five, yet it is these very challenges that made our union stronger, and we loved being parents.

However, my first pregnancy nearly did not come to fruition. After I got married, my lifelong best friend, my mother, started acting differently towards me and very cool towards Ian. Our relationship changed for the worst when we announced I was pregnant and she would be a grandmother. In 1989, six months into my first pregnancy she turned on me in a violent physical way. Let's just say that one morning turned into a scene from *War of the Roses*, with actors Michael Douglas and Kathleen Turner (Mom and I had a bitter divorce that day). I have shared the details in my third book, *Raise the Vibration Between Us* – however, it did not end well and I chose never to see or speak to her again after that.

When my dreams of being an architect faded, accounting took its place and I became a certified accountant. Once I received my designation, my career skyrocketed. Both Ian and I moved up the corporate ladder, almost in unison, from supervisor to manager to executive, over 16 years. Despite full-time careers, the family was always first, and we had a family tradition of eating breakfast and dinners together, no matter what. However, somewhere along my career path, I got caught up in 'titles' and corner offices and jet-setting across North America with Presidents and CEOs. I lost sight of our family tradition and my family took second place after my job. I started missing their sports games, musical events, and other moments that can never be recaptured. On many nights I called home to tell the kids I would be late for dinner. I remember one evening, in the fall of 2002, I was still at the office at 8 p.m., having arrived at 8 a.m. Shifting my chair for the cleaner to vacuum around me, I called home and said, "Hi, I am leaving work now I will see you…" My second daughter abruptly cut me off with a sharp reply, "You don't need to call us, we know you will be late, you are always late and maybe you should *stop* calling to tell us that every night." Click, she hung up.

What? Wow! I immediately felt a slap in the face and a cold blade sink into my heart. Out of the mouth of babes, her words stung me deeply and my eyes started filling up with tears. I had a good cry and then I sat there, dumbfounded. I looked around and there was no one in sight. Then it happened, slowly but surely, I began to look at myself with a different lens and from a different angle. The 'why' questions began bubbling up inside me.

Why the hell am I the last one to leave and the first one to arrive here every day? Why am I obsessed with replying to 150 daily emails so my inbox will be empty before I go home? Why am I working 60–72 hours per week every week!? Why do I have a family if I am never at home to see them or be with them? Why?

I didn't know it at the time, but my daughter's words would become a catalyst for changing my relationship with my career and my outlook on life in general.

The next day at the office my staff saw a new boss. Instead of diving into my emails first thing, I walked around the office, had conversations, and checked in with everyone. I made every effort to only check emails three times a day, turned off all sound notifications, and regained some peace of mind. I set a phone alarm for 4:30 p.m. to remind me to shut down my computer. I spent the last half hour of my day exactly like the first half-hour…I walked around the office, had conversations, and checked in with everyone. Staff and managers alike were shocked to see me at the elevator at 5 p.m. leaving for the day. As the grip of my former workaholic self, started to loosen, I found myself asking more and more questions.

As the weeks passed, I began to realize that I had done all the things I wanted to do: I was at the top of my career as a Finance Director, we had built our dream house from one of my architectural designs, I had three beautiful healthy children, all doing well in school, and a loving husband and father to our kids. What more could a girl ask for? Yet my life began to feel anti-climactic in virtually every way. I was only 38 and wondered had I accomplished everything I set out to do? Is this all there is? Now what? I had a feeling of finality and it felt strange. All my life I had lived like I was on a mission, to get this or the other accomplished, and now my to-do list was blank. I began to withdraw from my life and started going through the motions at work and home like an actor on a stage…I simply played my role.

Have you ever experienced a moment in your life when you became detached? You felt empty, hollow, or completely numb to everyday living – like a part of your life lost its meaning? And you asked yourself the question, *Why Am I Here*?

It's a question I began to ask myself on Christmas day of 2002 when my first life began to unravel. I felt empty inside, like a tree that had been uprooted – just a hollow shell of my former self. This feeling of emptiness affected me physically as well, so much so that when the dinner table was all set with a stuffed turkey, mashed potatoes, steamed vegetables, green salad, and the like, I looked across the table and what I saw looked like rocks and twigs. I didn't want to eat anything. I wasn't hungry. I suddenly had an intense feeling that forcing myself to eat was somehow a violation!

A violation of what I didn't know, at the time. I started questioning this concept of eating. Are we eating because we are socialized to believe we must eat three times a day? Are we hungry for food? I sat there quietly, watching my family eat Christmas dinner, and simply twirled some lettuce and cherry tomatoes around my plate, hoping no one would notice I had not eaten a thing!

On Christmas day of 2002, I stopped eating meat, and a few weeks later I stopped eating bread, pasta, and other carbs. I remember Ian took me out for breakfast on Valentine's Day and he ordered my favourite – pancakes. When the waitress put the plate down, I just stared at it for a minute, then looked at Ian and said, "I cannot eat this."

"Dawn you are scaring me. You need to eat something. I need you to make a doctor's appointment and I will join you. We need to figure this out."

By Valentine's Day, I had stopped eating vegetables and fruits as well.

I reluctantly made the appointment and my doctor took all the standard tests. The results all came back within the normal range. Have you ever had that feeling of here we go again? My life was pretty uneventful for almost 19 years after the 'fight of my life' just before university graduation. Nonetheless, here I was experiencing yet another loss. Reflecting on my childhood and youth, after each unveiling, I was led to an awareness of sorts, some new insights into my abilities, my stamina, my outlook on life. Although many lessons didn't come to me until later, I now had a sense that this loss of appetite meant something. While I should have been panicked, and those around me were at times, I felt a sense of freedom, or perhaps it was a detachment that I had never felt before. After Valentine's Day, my only sustenance… my only meal for the next six weeks was drinking water infused with fresh-squeezed lemons.

During this time, I never felt hunger pangs or food cravings, I didn't feel weak, had no headaches, nothing. I didn't even lose weight!

One of the most profound changes I experienced between Christmas day and my last day, in addition to my loss of appetite, was this almost insatiable need to be outdoors. I craved being in the sun, feeling the warmth of the sun rays on my skin. I was guided to start sun gazing as well during this period, every morning at sunrise and every evening before sunset. I found myself waking up maybe two or three minutes before sunrise and walking outside to greet the sun. It felt joyful, natural. I also needed to breathe fresh air, not recycled air-conditioned air from my office. I started leaving the office at lunchtime and walked to a nearby park. We lived on an acreage so when I got home, I would stroll into the forest in our back yard. I would often sit outdoors amongst the Scotch pines and maple trees until sunset. I needed to spend a few hours outside *every day*. My body was yearning for a new energy source as I was certainly not getting my energy from food. I remember calling a good friend one day and telling her, "I think I am turning into a plant! I am literally living on air, sunshine, and water, and yet I feel perfectly fine."

Each time I encountered a bump in this road called life, I found myself having to accept my new circumstances and surrender my fears, my worries, even my disabilities to a higher power. I surrendered my ears, my eyes, my voice, my legs, and even my heart to a higher power.

What more could I give? Give up? Yet I felt I was being guided to surrender something, maybe everything this time. Everything in this material world became meaningless to me: food, money, sex, home, career, status, all of it.

And surrender I did.

Insights: A New Sustenance

I had no idea how long my loss of appetite would last, yet I had a deep-seated trust that this was how I was meant to be. I needed to be emptied. I needed to shed some false beliefs about what I 'needed.' I was being shown a new definition of abundance and this abundance had nothing to do with my bank account or the square footage of my house or what make of car I was driving. I was allowed to know that I could exist without food, without wanting anything from this material world. I was led to the realization that abundance is always available to us through nature and I was supported and surrounded by a new energy that could sustain me indefinitely: sunshine, water, earth, air. Each element was feeding me in its own way. I felt my body changing and becoming more receptive to nature. I remember one evening when I got home, it was cloudy, but I was in my happy place among the trees with my back leaned against the trunk of a pine tree. Rain fell and I remained under the tree, breathing in the smell of newly wet earth, hearing the unique melody of raindrops tapping on the leaves. I listened as the songbirds changed their tune while they looked for a dry place to perch. Like a tree, I rooted into the earth for energy, and once the clouds had passed and the sunbeams reappeared, I stretched out my arms like branches of a tree to feel the warmth of the sun once more. And like a tree, I learned to connect to these natural energy systems around me. I was well fed!

Reflections: My Greatest Joy

Years later as I trekked across Canada with my musical instruments and books, I would often stop in British Columbia at a local martial arts studio where I performed sound baths (groups gathered to listen to various high frequency and harmonic vibrations from instruments such as quartz crystal singing bowls, Tibetan bowls, Paiste gongs, etc.). The sensei and I hit it off right away from our first meeting and we would often meet a few hours before the sound bath event and have long talks about spirituality and conscious living. In addition to teaching martial arts, the sensei also taught courses on equanimity.

Equanimity is defined as neither a thought nor an emotion, it is rather the steady conscious realization of reality's transience.

Equanimity is about one's ability to remain neutral in thought and emotion without attachment, recognizing that all reality is temporary.

When I shared with him my journey of withdrawing from food, losing my appetite, and spending hours each day in the forest, he chuckled and said, "Maybe you were becoming a breatharian, someone who does not need food to sustain themselves."

Interesting concept. I had never heard of this before.

"One moment, I have something for you," he said.

He gifted me a copy of a text he had framed and placed on the wall behind his desk. It was from a book entitled *Journey to the West* by Wu Cheng'en (circa. 1500 -1580, Ming Dynasty), considered one of the Four Great Novels of Chinese classic literature. The novel is a mythical account of the journey of a Buddhist monk, Xuan Zang of Dang Dynasty (circa. 650 AD), who travelled on foot from the capital city of Chang'an to India and brought back Suttra (sacred Buddhist scriptures) to China.

Here is what the text said:

What is the greatest fire?

Greed

What is the greatest crime?

Hatred

What is the greatest sorrow?

Separation

The greatest sickness?

Hunger of the heart

And the greatest joy?

The joy of freedom

*Freedom from **desire***

*Freedom from **possessions***

*Freedom from **attachment** and **appetite***

How does one meet suffering?

*By pursuing **happiness***

Speak and act with a PURE heart and mind

*And happiness will follow you like a shadow, **unshakable.***

I thanked the sensei for his gift, which now resides in my home office, to remind me that my greatest joy is *freedom*.

I was empty. I wanted nothing. I felt free.

CHAPTER SEVEN

Freedom

Physical Death Unveils Spiritual Awakening

What I am about to share with you are excerpts from my personal 'Spirit Journal' which I began to write in on March 21, 2003 – the day of my spiritual awakening, and I continued those entries for almost 18 months.

March 21, 2003

Three months had passed since my appetite went AWOL on Christmas day. No appetite for food, my work, sex, money, nothing. My gradual withdrawal from this earthly plane came to a head, on what would become *the day I will never forget as long as I live.* It is the day I realized that I was no longer interested in speaking. I had lost all desire and interest to talk. So I made a conscious decision to stop talking. I equated speaking with making noise, ego-based gibberish, and a waste of precious energy. What was the point? So I simply stopped speaking.

Now you might be asking yourself, how is that even possible with a husband, three kids, and a full-time demanding career?

To this day, I still shake my head when I think about what happened or did not happen on March 21, 2003.

Through a series of synchronistic events, I found myself alone for most of the day. I made breakfast for everyone, in silence. I kissed my husband goodbye as he went off to work, and hugged the kids before they left for school, in silence.

Not a word was spoken.

I just smiled as they waved from the school bus. I drove to work and thanked God there were no meetings that day. I closed my office door halfway, and to my surprise, no one, not a single person, came by, knocked on my door, or barged in unexpectedly, which was often the case. When my office phone rang, I simply let it go to voicemail. When the clock struck noon, I grabbed my car keys, got in my car, and drove home, not advising anyone of when I would be back. I had enough playtime pretending to be interested in my work.

I spent the afternoon outside with our two dogs, in silence. I walked, sat amongst the trees (my happy place), and breathed in all the abundant energy around me. I felt eerily peaceful and calm. It was a perfect afternoon.

That evening I had the house to myself as my husband took the kids to basketball practise right after school, and then they stayed to watch a university basketball game after practice. *Perfect!*

The day had turned into a silent retreat. I ended my retreat by drawing a hot bath before retiring to bed.

The First Awakening

March 22, 2003 (spring equinox)

Shortly after midnight, I felt my body becoming stiff. There was a strange sensation in my lower back that was slowly but surely travelling up my spine. Inch by inch my back was getting tighter – it almost felt like the contractions during childbirth – but the tightness was in my back, not my belly. I started paying attention to my heartbeat as well because I could hear it slowing down as this tightness moved up towards the center of my back. I said nothing as my husband lay on his side, sound asleep. My heartbeat got slower and slower and I listened until I heard my last heartbeat.

I experienced no fear, I was simply curious. I waited patiently to see what would happen next. And like a balloon slipping out of a child's hand and floating towards the sky, I felt something slip out of my body and start rising above the bed. Then to my surprise, I spoke. The first words I had spoken in 30 hours crossed my lips. As I was floating out of my physical body, the words poured from my mouth like water – **God, fill me with your love**. I rose a little higher and just surrendered myself to the experience. Can you imagine feeling every cell in your body at the same time? I felt love pouring into every cell, an explosive tidal wave of love washed over every cell of my entire being. I felt love like I have never felt before, and I burst into spontaneous laughter manifesting as the loudest belly laugh I ever had in my life! The proverbial genie had finally escaped its lamp! I was floating and weightless and felt loved beyond description. The moment I stopped laughing though and became quiet, the LIGHT show began! At that moment I became nothing but LIGHT as far as I could see and beyond the horizon. I watched the endless plane of light particles in every direction and there I was in it, I *was* it. I was FREE, I was HAPPY – no, I was ELATED. Many have asked me what the experience felt like. The amount of love I felt in that moment was the equivalent feeling of seeing a newborn baby, times one million.

For a few moments, I experienced Oneness as I connected to every living thing on this planet – every person, every animal, every plant, every living thing past and present. It's a feeling I will never forget as long as I live. To experience Oneness was incredible as I realized everything is connected to everything. What does Oneness feel like? The best analogy I can give you is this…imagine three countries you would love to visit. Now imagine visiting all three countries AT THE EXACT SAME TIME!! Yes, it is mind-blowing, but that is what it felt like for me. I was EVERYWHERE and part of EVERY living thing at once as time stood still.

Freedom

I do not know how long I was away from my physical body. All I do know are the three things I became aware of as my consciousness returned to my physical shell, lying still in bed.

The first realization that washed over me as I returned was a smell. The sweet smell of jasmine flowers filled the room. I then became aware of a six-note melody being played very faintly, over and over. Finally, I remember being kissed on my forehead. Smell, sound, and touch welcomed me back before I even opened my eyes.

With my eyes still closed, my focus drifted to the music, a new melody to my ears. It was beautiful and soft and underpinned faint words that captured my complete attention. Six words were repeated and gradually the whispering voice got a little stronger and louder as if it were moving closer to my ears. In my ears, a loving voice whispered, "ALL YOU NEED IS WITHIN YOU," followed by a gentle kiss on my forehead, like a parent kissing a child. I opened my eyes to an empty room. There was no one there, at least no one I could see.

Was I really back? I thought it was a one-way trip. I slowly raised my hands to make sure it was really ME. I recognised the hands, but I felt strange. I slowly sat up, felt the heaviness of my legs, my torso, and I came to a standing position with some effort, and walked into the bathroom. I needed to look myself in the eyes, I needed assurance that I was back. I stared into my eyes in the mirror for several minutes. *Am I back? Dawn, is that you? What just happened?*

This marked the first day of my SECOND life.

Kiss of Fire

March 23 – April 6, 2003

Not all kisses are kisses I would soon discover.

I told Ian what I had experienced the night before and that I felt out of sorts. How do you process hearing that? As I was telling him about the LIGHT show, he started smiling.

"What is so funny?" I asked.

"I thought you turned on the bathroom light," he replied.

"Oh my gosh, you felt the light. Ok, so it was not a dream, after all, this did happen!" Relieved, I wrapped my arms around him in a big bear hug.

He then got all 3D-like and reminded me I wasn't eating and I should try to have something warm, maybe some soup. I declined. I still could not or did not want to eat. I needed to process what had just happened. I needed to be quiet. I returned to my room and rested most of the day.

Later that morning, I began rubbing my forehead where I had been kissed, right at my hairline. My skin felt a little strange and I found myself rubbing it throughout the day. By the next day, half my scalp felt strange, not painful, just kind of itchy. I decided to shampoo my hair, blow dry it, and wrap it with a silk scarf. Nothing improved and by the third day, my entire scalp was screaming for my attention. After shampooing my hair once more, I went to bed and had the strangest dream with strange shapes floating all around me. At first, I thought they were musical notes until I realized they looked more like hieroglyphs. Dozens and dozens of strange symbols floated towards me, towards my head, then they disappeared. The next night I experienced the same dream, with these symbols I didn't recognize floating towards me and they flew into my head. After three consecutive nights of the same dream, I was finding it difficult to focus and I was uneasy not understanding my nocturnal adventures. After that third day, a new event took place that almost brought me to tears. My entire scalp began to heat up and for the next nine days, I felt excruciating heat. It was like an inferno had consumed my entire scalp. I didn't know what to do or even how to talk to anyone about this. I stood in the shower that first evening and let the cold water run over my head for a few minutes, but nothing changed. When I explained to Ian how hot my head was, he asked me if I could be having hot flashes. Really? I am way too young, and besides, why is it only my head feeling hot and not the rest of me? He suggested I make an appointment to see my doctor. He felt helpless and so did I. I needed to come up with a plan B so I could get some sleep. I started putting two icepacks on my head and wrapped it all with a towel during the day. As one set of ice packs melted, I grabbed another pair from the freezer and placed the melted pair in the freezer. That is how the merry-go-round went for several days as I attempted to cool off my head. At night, I ran cold water on my head just before bed. That brought some temporary relief so I could fall asleep, however, I was up a few hours later when the inferno returned.

During my plight to find relief from the 'kiss of fire,' I started scrolling through a holistic wellness publication called Vitality

Magazine which is distributed across Canada. I flipped to the section which listed different businesses and practitioners. I relied on my intuition to guide me to a photo of someone who I felt was authentic and honest. Her name was Deb. I called her.

Here is how the call occurred, "Hello, I cannot tell you my name, but I need to ask you something. At night I am seeing these symbols and my scalp feels like it is on fire, I don't understand what is happening to me."

In a calm voice, Deb explained that I was getting attuned and these symbols were bringing me either new information or new energies. She told me to look up the word Reiki on the internet.

I obediently researched this word and called her back a few hours later.

"This Reiki attunement says you need a teacher to give you the symbols, but I don't have a teacher; this happens when I go to sleep."

Deb chuckled and said, "You *have* a teacher, it just isn't a physical one."

She gave me some other terms to research such as spirit guides and ascended masters. I thanked her for her time and for giving me some vocabulary. Despite my efforts, I couldn't find any reference to my head feeling like it was on fire, or how to cool it down, but I did find the subject of Reiki fascinating.

Time for a Cool Down

April 6, 2003

I was ready to throw a party when I woke up that morning and my head was finally back to a regular temperature. What a relief!

The Sword of Fire

April 7, 2003

Each morning, Ian typically woke up around 5:30 or 6:00 a.m. as he had an early start to his day and a one-hour commute to work. That gave me at least 45 minutes or so to enjoy some me-time before I had to get up and get breakfast ready for the kids. With Ian safely gone, I drifted back to sleep.

About 15 minutes later I felt a familiar sensation in my back, like a contraction slowly moving up my spine. Although this time it continued past my heart and moved towards the base of my skull. My body began to stiffen as the contractions moved past the base of my skull before a sudden burst occurred at the top of my head and a strange sensation cascaded down my body, from my crown to my toes. It was almost *orgasmic*. Instantly, I felt a strong current shoot up through my skull. I was speechless as I witnessed my body split in three as that intense current surged through me. What the *%(&$@#! I tried to grab the sides of the mattress because I needed to hold onto something, as its force ripped through me with ferocity. At one point, the strong pulsing sensation felt like Niagara Falls was pouring into my crown. I do not know how long this lasted as it felt like an eternity, but I do remember watching myself retract like an accordion from three bodies back to one. I immediately placed my hands on the top of my crown as the surge suddenly stopped. *What the hell was that?* My heart raced so fast and I felt disoriented like I'd been tossed around in a tornado. I remained laying down for a few minutes until I finally caught my breath and sat up. *That was not a dream, no way.* I planted my feet firmly on the floor and began to stare out the window beside the bed.

God, why is this happening to me?

Please tell me what you want from me?

As I stared out the window, I realized there was a familiar scent of jasmine in the air and I put my complete focus on that beautiful scent. I closed my eyes and breathed it in slowly, to calm my nerves. As I began to calm down, a warm sensation emanated from my navel, or rather just slightly below my navel. I felt another sensation above my navel, almost like a cool breeze moving round and round. It felt pleasant, soothing. Then another warm sensation permeated my heart and I started to weep, as my heart flooded with love once more. I looked down the front of my body as I watched my T-shirt move ever so slightly out from the centre of my chest. I felt the most beautiful sensation spinning around my heart and it began to expand in the front of my chest and the centre of my back. I let the tears flow where they needed to go. My heart felt four times bigger — from the intense feeling of love pouring into me. I was reminded of the first words I spoke a few weeks before, God, fill me with your love. My request had been answered. I didn't know what had happened at that moment, but I felt that some part of me that had been closed, was now open. What had been empty was now full. Reflecting on the past three months, I realized that I needed to be emptied, to create space so I could be filled. I felt new sensations on and around my body that I had never felt before. That evening I wrote in my journal:

AS THE SEALS BECOME BROKEN, THE VEILS LIFTED, AND ILLUSIONS FADE, WHAT REMAINS IS THE REALIZATION THAT WE ARE CREATIVE, INTELLIGENT, LOVING, DIVINE VIBRATIONAL BEINGS HERE TO TEACH, LEARN, GIVE AND LOVE.

Insights: Kundalini

A full kundalini awakening is a specific energetic experience whereby it is believed that all the knots and issues of the psyche have been cleared or resolved. It's extraordinarily rare. More common is a partial kundalini awakening, where some of the chakras are activated or cleared. During a full awakening, a surge of energy rises from Muladhara or the root chakra up the back of the spine, over the top of the head, culminating in the forehead. The whole system awakens. Kundalini transforms on a physical, emotional, mental, and spiritual level. The natural evolution of the human being is to awaken to higher levels of consciousness.

When kundalini awakens, a person may experience deeper empathy with others, and this empathy can almost become telepathic. There is greater sensitivity, higher energy levels, sometimes psychic abilities or deep knowing, ageing can appear to slow down, creativity and charisma can increase, as can internal peace and knowing. There is a sense of being part of All that Is. The greater mysteries of life are no longer mysteries.

Time to Pray

April 8, 2003

I listened to Ian's suggestion and went to see my doctor. She was Egyptian and to my surprise when I found the courage to tell her what was happening to me at night, she received it well.

She told me about the priests in her village and how when they could not physically reach someone to assist them, they had out-of-body experiences and healed people that way. It was a common practice among the priests. I have to say, nothing about what she told me felt common and I could hardly believe that my doctor was not alarmed and was taking this in stride. It both reassured and bewildered me as she recommended I visit a priest at a nearby Coptic church, which is an Orthodox Christian faith out of Egypt, Africa, and the Middle East.

I obediently complied and drove to the church. The service was still going on, so I sat at the back and waited. I didn't have a clue what the priest was saying, however, I sensed when the service ended and most people got into a line in front of him, I thought it was to say thank you before they left. I followed suit and made sure I was the last person at the end of the line. One by one they greeted the priest and left and as the line got shorter, I wondered what I was going to say to him. When my turn finally came,

I made sure to look around as I didn't want anyone (and I do mean anyone) to hear what I was about to say to a man I never met before. I leaned over and whispered about my situation. I told him about my crown on fire, the light show, and my heart feeling so large. He said but two things to me:

"The Holy Spirit is within you."

"Remember, even Jesus went to the temple to pray."

He added, 'you must pray' as he placed a small prayer book into the palm of my hand.

As I drove home, I reflected on this concept of prayer. Although I was baptized twice (Catholic and Anglican), I was not a Sunday school girl. My mom was a person of faith and she prayed regularly but we did not attend church as a rule; maybe twice a year at Christmas and Easter but that was it. I often asked her why we didn't attend church more often, and her answer was always the same.

"Church is in your heart Dawn, not a building," as she pointed to her heart.

I never read the Bible or sang hymns other than in Catholic elementary school when we had to get ready for confirmation. Given my situation, what did I have to lose? I desperately needed something solid to hold onto before I completely lost my mind! Perhaps this little book would help me to stop feeling like Alice in Wonderland meets Morpheus from The Matrix.

I guess you could say I was an obedient child. I didn't give my parents any drama growing up. I was a 'good girl.' Well, almost a good girl. There were a few years when I drank while attending high school. Remember I was shy, especially going to parties and dances and meeting boys. Yes, I confess, I took a sip now and again to take the edge off from being shy. Sometimes I took more than a sip to numb the pain. **If you are an empath, I know you can relate to what I am about to say:** High schoolers have more heightened emotions than elementary school kids, and when I found myself in a high school of thousands, walking the corridors getting energetically bumped around like I was in a pinball machine, bumping into some heavy emotional energy – aka feeling others' fears, pain, and insecurities six hours a day – started causing *me* pain. Alcohol was my way of numbing the pain and turning down the volume on my empathic abilities during my high school years. It was the only way I knew how to handle the energetic predicament I was exposed to five days a week. My sobriety finally came about when I started university at age 16. Thank goodness for supersized lecture halls and endless open spaces to sit, eat, and study. No more feeling O.P.P. (other people's pain). I stopped drinking during my first year of university.

My life had been on an even keel except for those earlier bumps in the road. Yet here I was, 38 years old, feeling completely lost, like a baby placed in a jungle, without a flashlight or compass or GPS. I needed to find something to keep me sane as I was questioning reality. I questioned what was real – my waking hours or my dreams and visions. I questioned why I came back and what was I to do now. I was living in two worlds – the physical and the spiritual – and each one had its challenges.

When I arrived home, I opened the little prayer book. There were instructions to pray not once or twice but six to seven times a day! After my spiritual awakening, I had quit my job and I was home full-time so that wouldn't be difficult for me. I began praying at 6 a.m., 9 a.m., noon, 3 p.m., 6 p.m., and 9 p.m. There was a midnight prayer, but I chose not to stay up that late as I had three young kids to get off to school each morning. I was pleasantly surprised that after just a few short days I began to find comfort saying the prayers. The words took on a whole new meaning to me. Saying prayers was like a new language however, I quickly found a way to translate the words so that they made sense to me and my newfound experiences.

There is one prayer that took on a whole new meaning for me. Remember, these were the words my mom prayed after my horrific struggle to fully return to my body after an astral projection experience.

Psalm 23 KJV

²³ The Lord is my shepherd; I shall not want.

² He maketh me to lie down in green pastures: he leadeth me beside the still waters.

³ He restoreth my soul: he leadeth me in the paths of righteousness for his name's sake.

⁴ Yea, though I walk through the valley of the shadow of death, I will fear no evil: for thou art with me; thy rod and thy staff they comfort me.

⁵ Thou preparest a table before me in the presence of mine enemies: thou anointest my head with oil; my cup runneth over.

⁶ Surely goodness and mercy shall follow me all the days of my life: and I will dwell in the house of the Lord for ever.

My interpretation, given my situation and spiritual experiences:

Align with your highest self/God/Divine Creator/Source, and you will not want for anything (you are free).

Dwell in your heart (aka green pastures for the heart chakra).

Keep an even disposition and neutral emotional state (still waters).

Realize God within you; be godly in thought, word, deed.

There is nothing to fear when you walk in love, with love, and with faith (rod and staff).

You will always be provided for. Abundance comes to the anointed who remains connected to the highest self/God/Divine Creator/ Source (anointed head).

Goodness and mercy to those with a PURE and loving heart where they dwell.

Kissed by an Angel

April 14, 2003 - Palm Sunday

It was early morning and we were lying in bed. I felt a kiss on my forehead, and I heard, "no fear, no pain, all is love."

"Ian? Ian what did you…" I look over and he was sound asleep.

"Who said that?" I felt my forehead where I was kissed on my third eye this time. I knew that deep male voice, it sounded familiar.

Reflection

I had heard that same voice once before, a long time ago. I might have been 11 or 12 years old as my dad and mom were still married.

My parents had a weekly ritual of going grocery shopping every Saturday evening. On that particular Saturday, I was dressed and anxiously waiting to go out, sitting on the stairs between the first floor and second floor of our two-story townhouse. My dad came down the stairs and passed me to put on his shoes, then opened the door and went to start the car. My mom followed, and when she got to the front door and touched the doorknob, I stood up and suddenly realized that my feet couldn't move.

She turned to watch me on the stairs and asked, "Are you coming down?"

There I stood, frozen in time, my feet glued to the stairs. I felt my lower jaw move and the words flowed out gently, "I don't want to go." As soon as I heard those words coming out of my mouth, my first thought was, *what did I just say?!*

Mom then asked me, "Are you sure?"

SIT DOWN! That same deep male voice shouted in my head, "SIT DOWN!"

I felt increasing pressure pushing down on my shoulders. My knees finally buckled to the downward pressure and my butt hit the steps. I repeated the same phrase in a monotone voice, I don't want to go. She accepted my answer and left with Dad on their 30-minute drive to the store.

When the sound of Dad's car motor faded from my ears, I felt the downward pressure on my shoulders finally lift away. I stood up and walked down the stairs. Most Saturdays, we would finish grocery shopping within an hour. But I would soon come to realize that this was no ordinary Saturday. It had been three hours since my parents left without me. To calm my nerves, I began pacing up and down the kitchen where I could peer through the window to our parking spot in front of our townhouse.

Three and a half hours went by. Then came a knock at the door.

"Who is it?" I asked.

"It's officer so and so [*sic*], is this Dawn? Your parents are hurt, and you will need to come with me."

I was home alone, possessed a vivid imagination, and had watched more than my fair share of police shows. I asked the officer to walk over to the kitchen window and show me his badge, which he willingly presented. I asked him to wait outside while I called my godparents to tell them what had happened and that a police officer was waiting to take me to the hospital to see Mom and Dad. Luckily, my godparents lived nearby.

Within 15 minutes of the call, my godparents and I were sitting in the back of the police cruiser on our way to the hospital to see my parents. I can still remember my godmother's warm hands holding my hands as I sat nervously in the police car on our way to the hospital. I sat with her in disbelief when I heard the police explain that my parents were driving home when another vehicle in the opposite lane lost control and was heading towards them. To avoid a head-on collision, my dad swerved away from the oncoming car but ending up hurtling across two lanes, and his car flipped over into the culvert. Mom and Dad were both hurt and rushed to the hospital.

I sat in the back of the cruiser and looked around in disbelief, then I remembered the male voice shouting at me to SIT DOWN.

It struck me: *What if I had gotten into the car with them? There were no seat belts in the back seat. Would I have survived the car accident? Would I be alive today? Did that voice save my life?*

Although I felt lucky to be alive, I was never able to explain to my parents what had happened to me while I was on the stairs that night. I think I kept silent because of survivor guilt. I was okay but they had been hurt. I didn't have the vocabulary to explain what had happened, nor did I have any concept of angels – not back then.

Another time I heard the same male voice was in 2011. That time I was in a car driving and he saved me from a horrific car accident.

One morning, I drove my son to work. His shift started at 7:30 a.m. so, I typically dropped him off at work around 7:15 a.m., as I did on this morning before heading down the main street to get to the highway on-ramp. About a minute into my drive, a deep male voice commanded me to "PULL OVER FOR 10 MINUTES." Now my radio was off, and I was alone in my car. What would you do if you heard that? Trust the voice, I said to myself. I pulled over to the shoulder of the road, and I sat quietly, patiently, and obediently for ten minutes. When the clock said 7:26 a.m., I turned on the ignition and headed towards the highway.

I had barely driven three kilometres when I realized why the angel had told me to, "PULL OVER FOR 10 MINUTES." Ahead of me, was a collision involving a little silver car (the same make and colour as my car) with the front end partially crushed behind an 18-wheeler long haul truck. The accident had happened recently because no police car or ambulance had yet arrived on the scene.

However, the image I will never forget for as long as I live is the face of the driver as our eyes met. As my car drove slowly by and our eyes locked, he gently smiled as he saw my face — *he was smiling, and he looked relieved to see me! What?!* The expression on his face told me, "I am glad you are okay."

Was he real? Was I dreaming? Was he an angel? I looked ahead when I heard the ambulance siren approaching the accident scene. When I arrived home, I pulled into the garage, and sat there in silence for almost an hour! I tried to make logical sense of it all: the message, the time I received the message, pulling over for ten minutes, the accident on the highway, the man's facial expression, smiling at me.

Was he an angel? I don't know. But one thing I know for sure… when angels speak to me, I listen.

I have received several angel messages over the past 40+ years that have literally saved my life. Sometimes the angel message comes through my intuition, sometimes through my dreams, and more recently, I can hear them speak.

Too Much Information

April 17, 2003 - Full Moon

For the preceding nine days I felt like a satellite dish the size of a football field. I still felt connected to everyone, including the trees, the birds, our pets, and strangers. When the phone rang, I told my husband who was calling before he answered it. A former co-worker was pregnant and although I hadn't spoken to her, I just knew. Two months later she announced her pregnancy. I started dreaming I was reading newspaper articles, word for word, and within three to four weeks I began seeing the same news stories on TV. I felt pain from one of our two dogs. When I looked into his eyes, I could feel shooting pain coming from his head. I told Ian we needed to take him to the vet right away. The vet discovered he had a severe ear infection and needed immediate treatment. One evening, I was driving home and 2 km before I turned off the regional road to our street, I suddenly felt a stinging blow to the left side of my head. I was startled and pulled over to the shoulder. I rubbed my head, took a deep breath, closed my eyes, and tried to calm my nerves. From my third eye, I saw a deer lying down at the side of the road. I couldn't help but feel the deer was nearby. I opened the car door and began walking north. I walked about 200 metres and then I saw it. I felt queasy and held my stomach as I saw a buck lying in the culvert with blood oozing from the left side of his head. Tears flowed down my cheeks as I found the strength to walk back to my car. I called animal control before I resumed my drive home.

I began to avoid going into places with large groups of people, like the grocery store or restaurants, and sports games and movies were out of the question. I was overwhelmed by the impressions and information I was receiving – and it was unsolicited. I felt like the main character in that kids' TV series, *Harriet the Spy*. And while my crown chakra had not closed since April's kundalini awakening, my encounters with angels had magnified and I was receiving visions almost every night. I continued writing in what I now called my Spirit Journal, every day.

On this night of April 17, 2003, I was showered with visions of the past, present, and possible future, about myself, Ian, and my children. I cannot express how overwhelming it was to receive that many 'downloads' in one night. It was like trying to catch a fish with your bare hands as a school of them swim by your legs. I picked up snippets of things to come, but one vision came in so strong that I will never forget as it pertained to my next 'exit point' as the late Sylvia Browne used to call it.

In her book called *Life on the Other Side*, Sylvia Browne suggested that we have a total of five exit points in our lives in which we could leave this physical plane and return Home. Some of these exit points are obvious, like near-death experiences, serious accidents, or avoiding a potentially deadly event. Some exit points are more subtle, such as missing your flight and learning that the plane crashed or thinking you are late for work when you just missed a 10-car pileup on a patch of black ice.

The "other side" was the term used to describe a place our eternal spirits go to when we die. According to Sylvia Browne, the *other side* is our real home, a place we return to after our work is done on earth's physical plane. This book suggested that we are all here for a purpose and we all came to earth to learn lessons we planned to learn.

In my vision, I was riding across a vast stretch of land on a white horse. My head was partly covered with a shawl of some sort. My horse and I raced swiftly across the desert and from the corner of my eyes I saw lines drawn in the sand. There were long lines and short lines and I immediately interpreted the long lines as years and the short ones as months. I slowed down a little bit to count the long lines, so I'd know how many years I had left until my exit point.

I have had four exit points already: the car accident involving my parents when I decided (was told) to stay home; the attempted murder-suicide by my mother when I was six months pregnant; a near-fatal car accident the morning I dropped my son to work; and let us not forget March 2003. One more exit point to go. I know what year I will die (again). I will keep that to myself. There is only so much Ian can deal with. Between the sensations pervading my body, my intuition being on steroids, and my need to be celibate while I processed all this, it was more than I could expect him to handle.

I knew that I would at least see my three children grow to adulthood and maybe, just maybe, greet a second grandchild. It is a strange feeling to be aware that you are walking towards your death. Perhaps that is why I have consciously chosen to remain detached from this material world. I consider myself to be on vacation. I simply take things in stride as they come, positive or negative. After all, everything here is impermanent.

A New Way to Pray

Knowing what I know about my next exit point, I began to pray differently. I shifted away from the literal prayers to asking God for guidance. *Please show me the path to fulfil my destiny.* I know I came back here for a reason, and I know I only have so much time to do whatever I am meant to do this go-round.

I asked for guidance, and angels came during my prayers. Usually two, one male and one female, sometimes more. I was shown many things and I have received many messages, however not all angelic encounters were pleasant.

I remember one morning in May when Ian had left for work. I was lying on my side when two angels suddenly appeared. They caught me by surprise as I wasn't even praying at that time. I heard a strange sound coming from my chest and before I knew it, they swooped me up and I was outside and could see the roof of my house. Then suddenly, like a geyser I was catapulted straight up, moving almost at the speed of light. In mere seconds everything went pitch black and I thought, *where are we going?* Two more angels came to meet us. I was still disoriented from the speed at which we were travelling and was relieved we had stopped. I did a 360 and was shocked at what I saw. Off in the distance, I saw Planet Earth the size of a quarter. *Where are you taking me?* I felt tense and rushed and noticeably agitated. I wasn't ready to see what they wanted to show me. I resisted and was catapulted back in mere seconds with a heavy thump into my body to lie on my bed once more.

Jesus, I can't take this anymore!

For the first time I can remember in my life, I felt completely and utterly alone. I couldn't call Ian because he was at work. I couldn't talk to my kids as they were too young. I couldn't see my doctor as it would take days to get an appointment. My mother had long passed. I had no one to talk to. Feeling despondent and alone, I put my head back on my pillow and cried and cried.

Why, God, why? What do you want from me?

When the tears finally ran dry, I started thinking more clearly. I needed to talk to someone I trusted. In my heart, I knew who I needed...I called my dad who lived in the Caribbean.

"Daddy, I need you here, how soon can you come to Ontario?"

He told me he could come in two weeks.

Dawn, you must hold on a few more weeks, keep your shit together!

Thank God I wrote all this down in case I do go crazy because at least I have proof of what has been happening to me.

I continued to pray, do my candle meditation, and take lots of salt and lavender baths to calm my nerves.

Spiritual School

June 2003 – May 2004

A few days before my dad arrived, I had another angelic encounter. This time they visited me while I was in the bathroom. No privacy, I tell you. Two female angels descended and telepathically, I could hear them talking to each other. "Is she ready? She is ready."

Ready for what?

It turned out they were there to take me to school. They swooped me up only 10-12 feet from where I was sitting (someone got the memo that I didn't enjoy the last trip to outer space), and I found myself sitting at a desk in a classroom. Other students were there as well.

Over the next year, I attended many *spiritual* classes and received many lessons. Sometimes the teachers were male, others were female. For my first class, the message was short and sweet and the voice – that same familiar deep male voice – delivered it: **Good morning class. Today's lesson is God loves you.**

Some of the biggest spiritual lessons I received that first year were:

- *Live in the Light*
- *Stay aligned with your highest self*
- *Divine knowledge comes from within*
- *Forgive in all directions of time*
- *All you need is within you*

The Library and Readings

June 2003

My dad finally arrived at our place. I was thankful he could stay with me for a few months. Now my dad is not one to pack lightly and usually has overweight bags when he travels. This trip was no different except for *what* he had packed. One suitcase was full of books and cassette tapes. I had no idea my dad had so much spiritual knowledge. He brought me books on African spirituality, Egyptian spirituality, the Dogon tribe of Africa (a people with a propensity for knowledge about extrasolar astronomical bodies that could not have been discerned from naked-eye observation, such as the Sirius star system), a book on kundalini (also known as Serpent Power) and the Kemetic Diet (a program of conscious living that is based in the teachings and lifestyle of the ancient Africans who lived in Kamet, a land referred to today as ancient Egypt). Just as I realized later in life that my mom was very spiritual, I saw now that my dad was spiritual as well in his unique way.

My entire perception of my dad changed with this visit. Where once I was frustrated by his nomadic tendencies which made it difficult for me to set down roots and make lifelong friends, I now realized that his perpetual movement from country to country was about his insatiable curiosity and quest for knowledge. Now, I saw him not only as my father but as my first true physical-spiritual teacher. Between my full kundalini awakening and Dad's arrival, I was also hungry for knowledge and there were times I would pick out 10-15 books from the library and devour them in a day, and return the next day to take out another 10-15 books.

I wasn't so much reading them as scanning them, looking for specific topics, world religions (looking for a common thread), Reiki, kundalini, and concepts like the microcosmic orbit by Mantak Chia, the connection between Sanskrit language and sound. I found books by Barbara Brennan, Carolyn Myss, and Doreen Virtue, as well as ancient Chinese texts on immortality. For many weeks I felt like I was putting together pieces of a spiritual jigsaw puzzle however, someone forgot to give me the lid. Surprise!

My two older kids thought I was having a mid-life crisis. My youngest child though was the most attentive to what I was going through. I saw him now as an old wise soul and in time I would come to understand what his role in my life would be. During these past few months, my values and interests had drastically changed, and it was taking a toll on my marriage. As much as Ian was a great listener, he could not comprehend my experiences nor felt qualified to give me any guidance or support other than a logical solution – to see my doctor, eat more solid food, and so on. I could see he was relieved once my dad arrived as we both soon learned that Dad was almost a sage! My dad and I exchanged books and spent endless hours in discussions, philosophical and spiritual debates – it was amazing. I finally had someone I could relate to and who understood me and my recent experiences.

I had heard about a lady who lived nearby and had the gift of clairaudience – she could hear angels. I asked Dad to join me as I wanted to see her for a reading to help me put this jigsaw puzzle together a little faster. He was open to it and ended up getting a reading as well.

Her name was Abigail and during my reading, she was able to confirm my spiritual awakening in March through her communication with my guardian angels and her angels. At some point, I thought perhaps I had had a near-death experience, but I never travelled through a tunnel of light or saw any loved ones on any of my journeys out-of-body. Abigail went on to explain that approximately five years before, a critical mass of people started 'waking up' and that this group would affect the many, and that I am one of those people in the group.

Abigail had a gentle but also firm tone when she gave me these tips:

1) Do not astral travel without a purpose – remember that at age 19 you were almost possessed by an entity that left you paralyzed.
2) There is no need to protect yourself, as this in and of itself manifests fear. All you need is love.
3) You are most qualified to answer your questions, no one else; all you need is within you.
4) You are divinely connected to Source. Trust GOD to guide you in love.
5) You must learn to balance the spiritual and physical by grounding yourself.
6) There is no need to travel way out into the future. Find joy in the present moment.

I thanked her for her insights and tips, and Dad and I returned home. I am glad she wrote down everything as it was a lot to take in and remember. I still have her handwritten notes inside my Spirit Journal today.

Insights: Astrological Influence or Divine Timing?

As it turns out, a significant astrological event occurred in 2003, the same year of my awakening. The Total Lunar Eclipse of November 8/9, 2003, was the distinguishing feature in an exceedingly rare astrological chart that was highlighted by a six-planet alignment known astrologically as a "Grand Sextile." This picture of harmonically resonating planetary energies is expressed in a pattern that has been esoterically known for millennia as the Seal of Solomon or Star of David. In short, the symbolism embodied in this pattern speaks of ultimate balance, harmony, and unity. The spiritual/metaphysical import of this most unique arrangement of planets was the focal point of the worldwide celebrations of what has come to be known, globally, as the *Harmonic Concordance*.

The occasion was observed simultaneously at many hundreds of locations around the world. Some fourteen million like-minded individuals gathered, on the internet, in groups small and large, and in languages as diverse as we, to put out prayers of conscious intent directed towards the three salient points suggested by the chart's complex pattern:

- The descent of Creator Consciousness upon each individual
- The ideal of Unity Consciousness, that we are all ONE, and
- The creation of healing and protection for Mother Earth

Source: http://harmonicconcordance.org/

It is important to note that the influence of the Harmonic Concordance could be felt up to 12 months before the event and 12 months after. I woke up in March 2003 – eight months before the event.

Reflections: My Two Birthdays

Between 2010 and 2018, I attended dozens of holistic and health expos across North America. At one expo that I was a vendor at in Toronto, Ontario, I met an astrologer who also did palm reading. We had a 20-minute session at the expo, and I took his card as I wanted to get a full natal chart done. In fact, I wanted two charts. For a long time, I had asked myself why I woke up in this lifetime? Why had I spent so many decades living 'in my head' in a left-brain dominant career, only to leave it all behind and do a complete 180, now writing about conscious living, playing singing bowls, and doing energy work? I felt like I have lived at least five lifetimes since 1965 – with my career changes, my bumps in the road growing up as a child, and now this spiritual awakening that redefined my reality and what I wanted to do with my life.

I decided to get two natal charts done – one for my first life and one for my second life – and emailed the astrologer both my 'birth dates.'

A few weeks later, we met at his office in Toronto. I felt curious and excited to see what the charts had conveyed. First, he read my palms, and he picked up some daddy issues, understandably, especially after my parents divorced and I lost touch with him.

He also said I had something called the Ring of Solomon. It is a fine curved line under the index finger. It is said to symbolize knowledge and wisdom. The index finger (Jupiter's finger) represents our self-esteem, authority, power, ego, and leadership. It makes sense that the ring beneath the finger is impeding some of those qualities. Therefore, the person has a selfless and caring attitude with less focus on their own needs which allows insight into the nature of others. They have a gift for understanding people and are very intuitive. They often do counselling or social work.

After palm reading, he turned on his computer screen to show me the two charts.

"Now Dawn, I printed these out and I will go over them with you in detail, however, I need to show you this as I have never seen this pattern before."

"What do you mean?"

"I placed the two charts one on top of the other. Now, I want you to look to the left of the screen. The zodiac is divided into 12 segments or houses, and at the moment you were born, the planets were in a specific sign or house. The left side of the screen shows which house the planets were in, in 1965. Now, look at the right side of the screen. This shows which house the planets were in, in 2003. Do you see the placement of 12 dots on the left?"

"Yes."

"And on the right?"

"Yes, I see… it looks like a butterfly. They are almost a mirror image of each other!"

"Yes, exactly," he replied.

"What does that mean?" I asked.

"Well, that could mean that your awakening has marked a unique opportunity for you to experience the aspects of yourself that were dormant in your first life. Your logical, mathematical mind has taken a back seat in 2003 for your Divine mind to explore more subtle aspects, such as social, creative, and spiritual pursuits. In essence, this symmetrical phenomenon signifies completion, the complete balance of your life."

I remembered Abigail's message about the planetary event that took place in November 2003, bringing balance, harmony, and unity.

Triangles Within Triangles

Late June 2003

One night while I was sleeping in the basement, I had a dream about an emerald-green triangle. It appeared in my third eye, and a few seconds later a second one appeared. One triangle pointed up and another pointed down. Together they formed a six-pointed star. A third triangle appeared to join the other two, then a fourth. As each triangle intersected the other in what appeared to be a final pattern – a 12-pointed star was formed. I was guided to get out of bed and sit on the floor. With the sheet wrapped around me, I closed my eyes and recreated the 12-pointed star in my third eye. My mind became very calm and my body followed suit. After a few minutes, I could feel a gentle breeze swirling around me, yet I knew the windows were all closed. I felt comfortable in the middle of this enchanting breeze like I was in the centre of the Universe and I was untouchable. It felt blissful. I couldn't feel my body as I felt like I was in a bubble, floating away. In the distance, I heard the patter of little feet walking down the stairs.

"Mommy?"

I opened my eyes to see who it was, "Yes, honey." (It was my son, my youngest.)

"I don't want you to go."

"Baby, I am not going anywhere, why would you say that?"

"Can I stay with you?"

"Yes, come here."

I walked with him back to my sofa bed, where he lay in my arms and we fell asleep. I am not sure to this day what my son felt or why he thought I was leaving but in any event, I chose to stay.

Insights: 12-pointed Star

In time, and through meeting other Lightworkers and taking courses, I would come to know this image in my third eye was the 12-Pointed Star or Double Merkabah – for activating your light body and light codes and connecting you with the Higher Realms.

This sacred shape is a cosmic portal to the angelic gateway and the outer dimensions of our universe where information and wisdom are immediately accessible and rapidly integrated into our 3D human form. This sacred shape can be used to awaken you to higher levels of consciousness, including your own infinite wisdom. The 12 points of these stars also symbolize completion and wholeness.

Since my spiritual awakening, I have been guided many times to sit quietly on the floor, in lotus. In the stillness and softness of being fully present, without thought or anticipation, I receive insights into the nature of my spiritual abilities and my life purpose. In time I came to know the Merkabah as a method of infusing the highest vibrational frequency of light into my energy field and body (as humanly possible). It was not some action or practice that I did, but rather accepting an invitation to have an experience that left me feeling reborn and purified each time.

It is important to note that one cannot activate the Merkabah so that the Merkabah itself can assist you to reach other dimensions or ascend. Instead, the Merkabah "activates" on its own because of shifting consciousness. It is a symptom of increasing one's vibration of consciousness, not a cause of increasing consciousness.

The Merkabah "becomes alive" in response to a person's energy field and their ability to attain a higher consciousness, unrestricted by the limitations of the vibrational density of the physical dimension.

Two More Pieces of the Puzzle

July 2003

I remember my dad explaining to me that summer that I was connected to 'Source.' I sort of understood what he meant but I needed answers. I was still uncertain about what took place in March. Once again, I let my fingers do the walking, this time on my keyboard on the internet.

I found an ashram in Toronto and decided to visit them one Saturday afternoon. There I would meet Swami P. When he saw me enter the building he bowed and said, "Welcome." I eased into a conversation that ended up lasting two hours. He told me he devoted his life to the temple at age 23 and now 30 years later, he had experienced a partial kundalini awakening. We talked about the physical body, enlightenment, reincarnation, the spirit, and kundalini. I asked him what the purpose of kundalini is and what happens when all our chakras are open. He smiled and said, "Ahh, not everything is written in a book." Before my visit ended, he lent me a copy of the Gita and insisted on offering me some food. The Bhagavad Gita ("Song of God" or "Song of the Lord") is among the most important religious texts of Hinduism. Also called The Gita, it combines the concepts expressed in the central texts of Hinduism, the Vedas and Upanishads, which are here synthesized into a single, coherent vision of belief in one God and the underlying unity of all existence. The text instructs on how one must elevate the mind and soul to look beyond appearances – which fool one into believing in duality and multiplicity – and recognize these are illusions. All humans and aspects of existence are a unified extension of the Divine which one will recognize once the trappings of illusion have been discarded. I left with The Gita and some pieces of ginger cake and apples. The following day, I finished reading The Gita, lining the pages with yellow sticky notes, anticipating my next discussion with Swami P. On my next visit, we not only discussed The Gita but I was introduced to a new term Samadhi – which became a large piece of my puzzle and gave me some context around my spiritual awakening in March and some of the activities that followed. I continued to visit the ashram for almost a year and enjoyed relating to someone with whom I could share my spiritual adventures and who could shed some light on my new gifts and abilities.

Insights - Samadhi

Samadhi State is also known as Transcendence, an event where the body is separated from its soul. The meaning of the word Samadhi means "bring together" or "unification of mind." Samadhi is one such state of mind where a person can heal the karmas of their life. It is a state of Oneness – a perfect union of the individualized soul with infinite spirit.

Samadhi is said to be an experience of divine ecstasy as well as of superconscious perception; the soul perceives the entire universe. In other words, human consciousness becomes one with cosmic consciousness. The soul realizes that it is much more than the conditioned body. It is also known as the eighth and final step on the path of yoga described by Patanjali. Samadhi may be attained through deep, continuous, and correct meditation. In this state, the three aspects of meditation—meditator, the act of meditation, the object of meditation known as God—are finally united.

Captivated by Crystal Sounds

September 2003

I decided to study Reiki and thought maybe this was what I was meant to do. After all, I had received many attunement symbols back in the spring when I woke up. Whenever I was around people who were sick or in pain or suffering from severe stress, my hands would heat up and I naturally wanted to 'reach out and touch them', not an appropriate gesture when you are standing in line in the grocery store and intuit that the person in front of you has a major migraine. I enrolled in a weekend Reiki level one and two classes, and while I found the classes remarkably interesting, the real reason I went to them, however, was not realized until the last hour of our last day.

The six students and my Reiki teacher sat in a circle. She placed a large white crystal bowl in front of her. She led the sound circle with something called sacred vowel sounds, and we repeated the vowel sounds together once she pronounced the vowel. As we sang these vowel sounds, she played the white crystal bowl. I was captivated by the sound and vibrations I was feeling, and within five minutes I felt my aura expand in every direction about 50 feet from my body. Wow! It was an incredible feeling of joy and love – almost like my first awakening but without the light show. By the time we finished the sound circle, I was beaming and smiling from ear to ear.

"What did you do? And what is in that bowl?" I asked the teacher.

She showed me how she used the small stick around the rim to make the bowls 'sing.'

"Would you like to try it?" she asked.

"Yes, please."

It was heavenly and as they say, the rest is history. I bought my first crystal bowl the following week, added a second bowl the following month, and my little family of bowls would continue to grow. My Reiki teacher had given me a wonderful gift, rekindled my love for music which was now coupled with a love for healing others. I knew in my heart and soul that I was meant to heal others with sound.

For two years I was on a mission to learn all I could about sound healing. I studied practices from different cultures, ancient cultures. I came across some fascinating work by a sound healing pioneer named Fabien Maman, and his organization, Tama-Do Academy. He became a mentor for me as I developed my understanding of the connections between crystalline sound, the brain, spirituality, and our innate healing abilities.

One of Fabien's studies which I found fascinating occurred in the early '80s. Fabien conducted his revolutionary biology experiments at the University of Jussieu in Paris, showing the impacts of acoustic sound on human cells and their energy fields. Fabien found that through a series of acoustic sounds, he could explode cancer cells, as well as energize and empower healthy ones.

At the same time, I was enjoying Fabien's work, I came across Professor James Gimzewski at UCLA and a new word 'sonocytology' – which means the study of the sound of our cells. UCLA graduate student Andrew Pelling and Gimzewski published sonocytology's debut report in the August 2004 issue of Science magazine. In the sonocytology studies, a Bioscope AFM (atomic force microscope) was modified to be able to detect the vibrations of the cell wall of a living cell. These vibrations, once amplified using computer software, created audible sound, and it was discovered that cancerous cells emit a slightly different sound than healthy cells do. Gimzewski and Pelling hope that sonocytology may someday have applications in early cancer detection and diagnosis. Imagine the implications – to use sound as a non-invasive approach to reversing disease in the body and improving cellular health! I started to connect the dots of the amazing world of sound healing and the vibrational frequency of cells and our brainwaves.

Integration

My spiritual experiences continued with intensity for almost 12 months after my awakening, and I recorded 24 profound spiritual experiences that first year. This truly was a season of change. Most of my former business colleagues and acquaintances who wore suits and carried BlackBerry phones faded out of my life. I continued to meet Reiki practitioners, medical intuitives, angel and tarot readers, channelers, and astrologers, a whole new community that up until that point I never knew existed. I guess everything has its season.

In time, my heightened empathic abilities would calm down so I could enjoy going out and socializing in small groups. I was becoming more comfortable living in two worlds, the physical and the spiritual, as I was learning how to integrate them.

Instead of viewing my new gifts as a curse, I embraced them, and I consciously chose when to be fully open to Spirit and when not to. When I looked back at the past year, I reflected on how a large part of my journey and learning was divinely guided and experiential. Before I had met any physical teachers I had discovered my chakras and began belly and pranic breathing. I was guided to meditate with a candle which unbeknownst to me at the time, was a spiritual practice from India called Trataka, which was strengthening my inner vision capabilities. I began working with crystals, colour, essential oils, and nature. As a result, I changed the way I ate, how I spent my time, and how I communicated with others. I was consciously aware of frequencies that were beneficial for my health and frequencies that were not. I wanted to share what I had learned but I didn't know where to begin.

During my second year, and after countless times of asking God, what do you want from me, an answer came in the form of a question.

Dawn, what do you love doing?

It wasn't the answer I was expecting however, it was an answer all the same. I pulled out my journal and started writing down everything I loved to do. After I exhausted my list, I noticed a common thread in all the items. Whether I was teaching someone to play music, understand mathematical formulas, build a train set, ride a bike, use a computer program – everything I loved to do encompassed teaching.

I love to teach.

Then go and teach!

Finding My Way

In 2005, I began public speaking about the Power of Sound to Heal. I had returned to my love of music, however, instead of the piano, this time my instrument of choice was quartz crystal singing bowls and Tibetan bowls. That year, I began holding sacred sound circles that included meditation, toning and chanting, and playing the singing bowls. When I played the bowls I felt fulfilled. The ability to hold space for others to connect to their inner divinity and activate their innate healing abilities was only part of the joy I felt. It was also a time for me to fully open my spiritual side and recreate the feeling of Oneness. There is something magical and mysterious about how the vibrational tones of these instruments weave through and connect us into one beautiful energy field. The crystalline sound waves I also affectionately call my 911, as, within minutes of playing the quartz crystal bowls, my angelic guests fill the room and begin attending to the participants in deep need of healing. I have witnessed hundreds of miracles and blessings from angels as they work silently with others during my sound healing group sessions.

2005 was also the year I received a beautiful gift from the late Sylvia Browne. She gave me a message in a dream that ignited my quest to learn all that I could about vibrational frequency. Her one phrase, "it's all about frequency control," was the glue that held all my spiritual experiences together. I understood now that my frequency was elevated when I experienced Samadhi, and by vibrating at these higher frequencies it created the perfect environment to attract more spiritual experiences. My elevated frequency allowed me to feel, see, and hear angels. As my knowledge of the laws of vibration expanded, I became more confident in my ability to teach others how to raise their frequency and live more consciously.

In 2006, I created a workshop called How to Raise Your Vibration and took my little flipchart and singing bowls and started travelling across Ontario, and then neighbouring provinces. One day, Ian suggested I write down all the things I wanted to teach. I listed all the topics that I felt would benefit others. I had three categories related to vibrational frequency and conscious living. There were topics to raise your frequency (everything I learned and was guided to do the first year of my second life), topics to improve your home and work environment by detoxing the air, light, and water that you use as well as metaphysical and spiritual practices to keep your home calm, safe and comfortable. Lastly, there were topics about clearing karma, how to forgive, and how to improve the quality of your relationship with others and yourself.

When I reflect on my inspiration to write three books, I realize that each one spoke about harmony – living in harmony with yourself, each other, and the planet. My three-book collection is called the Raise The Vibration Trilogy.

The Trilogy

Raise Your Vibration, Transform Your Life:
A Practical Guide for Attaining Better Health, Vitality and Inner Peace (2010)

How to Raise the Vibration Around You:
Volume I: Working with the 4 Elements to Create Healthy and Harmonious Living Spaces (2014)

Raise the Vibration Between Us:
Forgiveness, Karma, and Freedom (2018)

Book one was well-received across the globe and that first book brought me many blessings as I travelled four continents, met thousands of people, and touched many hearts with my sacred sound healing circles.

At last, I was living in alignment: mind, body, and soul; doing what I love and loving what I do. After book three was published I thought, well it's done, the trilogy is complete and I did what I set out to do, my destiny is fulfilled – teaching others how to live consciously and harmonically. I was entering a new season of life, my sunset years as I affectionately call it. And I have had time to write one last book, *Unveiled.*

Time to Go Home

I have had an incredible journey, of living, loving, dying, awakening, and teaching. There was only one thing left to do, find the place my soul has been calling me to for over 50 years.

I believe this vision first occurred around age three and played over and over in my life for almost 50 years. I routinely travelled to this place in my dreams, while my body lay still on my bed, and found myself standing in front of the exact, same tree.

I like it here. I will stay awhile.

Look at the leaves on that tree. I have never seen leaves like that before. They play with the warm breeze, turning this way and that. It almost looks like a hand waving hello to me. My eyes roam upwards, higher than the tallest trees, and my attention is drawn to some fluffy white clouds, softly and slowly rolling by. I gaze at them until I begin to see shapes. I love imagining and seeing all those odd shapes, especially the funny animal shapes in the sky. The sun's rays kiss my cheeks. I smile. I stop daydreaming and my attention returns to the earth. Everything is a luscious shade of green. I return to tending to the animals. I am so excited as we just had a kid. I love baby goats. I pick up our new arrival. As I carry her to a bed of straw, I can feel her heartbeat and her warmth fills my heart with love.

I like it here. I will stay awhile.

Freedom

Thanks to a freak ice storm in Ontario in 2014, Ian and I decided to escape to a warmer climate and took our first trip to Costa Rica. We were empty nesters for four years and were acting like a couple of teenagers. We packed one backpack each and flew to San Jose without even a hotel reservation! By the second day of our arrival, we both realized that this was where we want to spend our retirement. We fell in love with the land, the people, the flora, the animals, the food, the music…all of it. By day six of our trip, we had retained a real estate agent. With our combined excitement we manifested a plan to relocate and after a few short years, we were living part-time in Costa Rica!

For the first time in my life, I have found peace with *being at peace*; enjoying moments of stillness, silence, and *living in harmony with myself*, nature…life. It feels like a summation of a long journey and a realization of the vision that I had when I was three. At last, I found my soul's home away from Home.

And what of that tree in my vision?

Who knew that I would find that tree right outside our living room window, but then again, perhaps it was already there waiting for my arrival. It is called the guarumo tree, native of Costa Rica, and sloths love to hang out there.

And what about the goats?

A few months after we arrived, Ian installed some farm fence and surprised me with three new four-legged pets: two female goats and one male ram. Rumour has it one of the females is pregnant (smile). Ian's nickname became 'Farmer James' when he started a hobby farm years before back in Ontario with chickens, ducks, turkeys, and some four-legged animals. It turns out that having goats was something he had been dreaming about as well.

It has been a wild ride and I am eternally grateful for my two incredible lifetimes which were filled with many monumental events, some of which almost took me to my breaking point. Had it not been for the resilience instilled in me by my parents, I do not doubt that I would not have had the fortitude to survive. Looking back, it was fortuitous that I had these two uniquely spiritual parents who both gave me the space I needed to find my path, yet when I needed their guidance and support the most they were there. For that, I am eternally thankful to them and my husband and children who have spent many lifetimes with me.

My life has been a series of tests and trials, from being temporarily blind, deaf, paralyzed, and more. Each one of these life events presented an opportunity to surrender to something greater than myself. At times I wonder where I found the faith, trust, and strength to make it through. I am thankful that as I passed each test, a veil dropped revealing to me new aspects of my humanity and divinity. The final test required me to surrender everything. I was asked to empty myself and ultimately to leave my body behind. In return, I was able to see behind that final veil, to experience the light of Oneness, and chose to return so that I might experience all aspects of me (mind, body, soul, and spirit). My empty vessel has now been filled and the lessons from each unveiling, fully integrated.

What Am I?

I am All that Is, expressed as a spiritual being that is currently on vacation as Dawn James.

Who Am I?

I am an Awakened One who chose to return.

And the lines in the sand, marking my next exit point?

I am simply walking toward another chapter and through another veil. See you on the other side!

Connect with Dawn

Visit her website for products, services, and resources at
dawnjames.ca

Join Dawn for high vibration experiences at
SoulfulHealingRetreats.com

Ready to share your story?
Let Dawn show you how at **PublishandPromote.ca**

Other Books & Audiobooks by Dawn James

Raise Your Vibration, Transform Your Life (English, Spanish)
https://www.amazon.com/Dawn-James/e/B003BAIT7W

How to Raise the Vibration Around You
https://www.amazon.com/Dawn-James/e/B003BAIT7W

Raise the Vibration Between Us
(English, Spanish, French, Hindi)
https://www.amazon.com/Dawn-James/e/B003BAIT7W

Raise the Vibration Between Us (audiobook)
https://dawnjames.ca/raise-the-vibration-between-us-audio/

Why Are We Here (audiobook)
https://dawnjames.ca/why-are-we-here/